CH00828331

PRAISE FOR
AND *The An*

"I believe that Tobin is the next Adyashanti or Eckhart Tolle. The sheer awakening presence of sitting in his meditation groups is awesome. One comes away not in awe of another teacher but actually awakened somehow in the mystery and aliveness and beauty of one's own presence. This is a true teacher, who can transmit directly a deeply established state that took many years of hard work and reflection and make it seem so effortless to fall into the silence and presence."

~ELIZABETH R.

"I have known Tobin for nearly two decades, and watched his growth and development as a therapist, writer, teacher, and enthusiastic supporter of others' growth. I have great admiration for his diverse range of skills as a therapist, creativity as a conveyor of spiritual dharma, and deep care about human beings and supporting their potential in creative and intelligent ways. Anyone would benefit from his work!"

~MARIANA CAPLAN, Professor of Transpersonal and Yogic
Psychologies and Author of *Eyes Wide Open,*
Halfway Up the Mountain, and *Do You Need a Guru?*

"Tobin has a rare ability to be fully present: to listen intently to the spoken word, read the body language, feel the energy, take it all in. With careful consideration, he shares with each of us his wonderful words of wisdom and well-grounded advice that serve to gently nudge us forward, one step at a time, on our individual paths of personal growth and spiritual development. Always patient, always kind, always there, his guidance is like a beacon of light on a stormy night helping us to navigate the often tricky and unpredictable waters of life."

~COURTNEY K.

"I have been continually touched by your presence and the sweet deep satsang space that you hold. You elicit love. You open the doors to delicious, full, still ground. You call hearts home. Something about what you create inspires me in a big big way. Thank you."

~CHLOE G.

"I am eternally grateful. Your love, compassion, understanding, wisdom, guidance and openness have helped me truly get in touch with the essence of who I am. My life has gently unfolded in such a beautiful manner since I met you and I don't know another human being who could have so delicately brought this about. It feels like a miracle."

~PIPPA G.

"I have accomplished more in six months working with Tobin, experienced more depth of healing, growth, and movement in my life, than in 20 years of psychotherapy. He is uniquely gifted and skilled at zeroing in on the sticky places, then applying his wisdom, insight, and tools to effect change. He is able to focus on and help heal the troubled areas with a kind of laser-like (but very gentle!) precision more often used to describe surgeons. I feel very blessed and lucky to have found him!"

~NANCY LEVINE, Author of *The Tao of Pug*

"How do you express gratitude to a soul for bringing light back into a wounded heart? My aloneness melts in the light of your generosity. Your spiritual transmission is Technicolor! You're loved forever for your graceful gifts."

~SAM C.

"Working with Tobin has had miraculous effects on my life. He gave me a way to not only manage my own thoughts and emotions, but to actually use them to heal the layers of wounding that they arise out of. My marriage, my health and my life have all been transformed."

~DANA N.

THE ART OF

MINDFUL
LIVING

THE ART OF
MINDFUL
LIVING

YOU CAN'T STOP THE WAVES
BUT YOU CAN LEARN TO SURF

TOBIN GIBLIN

ZENTREPID
PUBLISHING CO.

ISBN 978-1-4276-5094-8

Book design by Liz Siverts

This book is dedicated to anyone who might be served by it.
May You Awaken to the Truth of Who You Really Are.

CONTENTS

PART ONE
THE ESSENTIAL INGREDIENTS

PART TWO
WORKING WITH DIFFICULT EMOTIONS

PREFACE

As I sit atop this cliff overlooking the beautiful expanse of sea and sky, two hundred feet or so above the ocean, I am in awe and gratitude for this moment of being alive. The waves role in endlessly, seemingly from an infinite nowhere in the distance. I feel the wind and sun on my body and hear the crashing of the ocean against the rocks below. Birds sing their songs of celebration.

Sitting here, I am once again reminded of the power of the ocean and its unpredictable, awesome nature. The waves are always rolling in. As I look closer, it seems as if there are waves on top of waves on top of waves. My awareness expands and I feel myself here — in this ocean I call "my life" — and I am struck by the power of the currents flowing in me and around me, even in this most tranquil of moments. Some of the waves are obvious and strong; others are subtle and under the surface. My memory kicks in, and I remember the recent and distant past experiences that felt more like tsunamis in comparison to this peaceful summer morning. I see more clearly than ever that my entire existence is floating in and consisting of these waves — both the smaller ripples of my moment-to-moment experience and the larger tidal movements that my journey is unfolding within. In this moment, I feel the waves of my breath, the sensations flowing through my body, my emotions, my thoughts . . . and, at the same time, I sense the larger currents that my life is swirling in: my relationships, my body's states of health and well-being, my age, my finances, my current work situation, all of my life's circumstances.

Regardless of our current situation, our personal experience is floating in this wild and often times tumultuous, miraculous ocean of existence we call life. Every person is alive in this mystery, riding waves of untold numbers and kinds at every moment. In this book, I offer a basic orientation for riding these waves — for "surfing" this ocean of existence — in a way that is the most skillful and, ultimately, the most natural to us. These simple instructions — ones you may have heard before in different forms — are presented here in a manner that has given many people, both those new to mindful awareness and those seasoned on the path, a straightforward and user-friendly way to meet life's undulations artfully.

Each chapter illuminates an aspect of the true nature of our unconditioned awareness or elucidates practices to help dissolve the main barriers to abiding as that open space of consciousness that we fundamentally are. The first ten chapters present the various qualities or underlying "attitudes" inherent to the unconditioned state of our awareness. In the same way that a prism allows one to see the various colors embedded in white light, these chapters help to lay out in front of us, one by one, the underlying subtle aspects of how our ordinary, everyday awareness orients to what flows through it. We are invited here to realign ourselves with these aspects, thereby connecting once again to the healing and transformative power available to us as human beings. In part two, we are instructed and given the encouragement to meet the more challenging waves of our journey in the most noble, skillful, and fruitful way possible.

Each of the chapters is a transcription of a talk that I gave in Mill Valley, California, over the course of several years. These were the talks that I found myself giving again and again, as new students would join the group and as I could feel that even the more devoted among us needed booster-shots of the most crucial aspects of the practice. At some point, it made sense to collect these foundational pieces into one easily readable manual. This inspiration was the birth of the book you are now holding in your hands.

Reading the chapters in order will unveil for you, step by step, the most foundational and important understandings of a skillful mindfulness practice. The later chapters put all these aspects together and help us apply this art form to the most difficult part of our everyday existence: the emotional waves that continually flow through us. I encourage you to read the book once the entire way through. Then, if you wish, revisit it in any way you find inspiring, uplifting, or reminding. Many readers have told me that they really "got" the deeper gifts of what this simple book has to offer on the third or fourth read-through or when something inspired them to reread a specific chapter after months of not looking at the text at all.

The words that follow come directly from a deep wellspring of presence and are simply pointing back to that source. I hope that you find these words encouraging, uplifting, and, most of all, useful. They are intended to clarify, elucidate, and perhaps fine-tune the invaluable skill of being aware and present within this very moment of our precious existence. This simple yet subtle art allows for our journey to unfold in the most optimal way, ultimately revealing to us once again the beauty, majesty, and miraculous nature of the life we are living right Now.

I see this book as a gift. It has been a gift to me to write it and to share it. Many people have expressed that it has completely changed the quality of their lives. My sincere hope is that you receive the invitation that it offers and find your way through the limiting veils of conditioning and into an authentic, embodied experience of the true nature of your existence. This is the miracle that mindfulness has to offer.

TOBIN GIBLIN

Big Sur, California

June 2011

PART

ONE

THE ESSENTIAL
INGREDIENTS

Skillful mindfulness practice is about aligning
ourselves with the qualities of our True Nature,
the one and only source of the fulfillment we all seek.
The following chapters are designed to help create
a balanced foundation for your journey
to this fulfillment.
May You Be Guided Home.

CHAPTER ONE

THE IMPORTANCE OF NOW

Let your brain whirl and spin itself
into blessed and exhausted silence.
Let it rest like a baby in the
open palmed hands of the heart held Now.

ADYASHANTI

One of the most essential understandings on which all mindfulness practice is based is that there is only NOW. Only Now is real.

It is not difficult to realize this fact. Just look to your direct experience. What actually exists? Only what is happening in this moment . . . right? If you observe closely, you see that the future and the past do not fundamentally exist. They are simply figments of your imagination projected onto the movie screen of your mind. And even that is happening Now.

The path of mindfulness is based on the fundamental truth that reality is an ever-unfolding flow of sensations, thoughts, feelings, sounds, sights, and tastes that is always taking place in the present moment. Therefore, what we practice, both in formal meditation and in the moments of our everyday life, is — as Ram Dass so succinctly recommended — to simply "Be Here Now."

The essence of mindfulness practice is actually quite simple. In a nutshell, it is about remembering to be in the present moment, landing in the direct experience of our life as fully as possible. All we have to do is to put our attention on what is happening in our experience — Now.

Unfortunately, however, anyone who attempts this practice soon realizes that even though it is simple, it is not one bit easy — especially to do in a sustained way where we can reap the benefits of what mindfulness truly has to offer. The mind has a very "slippery" way of staying out of the present moment. Instead, it tends to dream its way into the future, slide into replaying the past, or sit back and judge whatever it doesn't find perfectly to its liking. The mind is constantly spinning out a completely false life based on these habits of thought and the imagined identities that go along with them. This is an age-old and incredibly powerful habit!

When we finally do land in the present moment, another profoundly daunting challenge presents itself. What we often find is some degree of physical or emotional pain in our body. Either on the surface, or lurking somewhere underneath, we find physical discomfort, frustration, anger, grief, fear, tension, and other sensations of unpleasantness. These pain-layers are exactly what we are trying to avoid by not being present. And yet, in the process of trying to avoid our pain, we are paying a huge price: We are losing connection to the immediacy of our life and thus to the source of all the true joy and contentment that we are capable of experiencing.

That's where the *Art of Mindful Living* comes in. In this book we will discover the skillful means of reconnecting to that place where all true satisfaction and fulfillment can be found. Surprisingly, this "place" happens to be right here in your body, right here in this very experience that you are having . . . in this very moment.

The fact is, everything we are searching for is always right here in each and every one of us, as the very substance of us! At every given moment, there is a pool of peace, love, bliss, joy (and whatever other wonderful quality you can imagine) in the very fabric of our very own "Being" — right NOW. In the immediacy of this moment, we can discover the essential nature of who and what we are, and we can awaken to the joyful realization that this "Essence" is what we have always been searching for.

So, mindfulness practice is about remembering to be in the present moment, being aware of the very experience you are having right now. That's all. You don't need to let your mind get over-involved in the attempt to Be Here Now. You don't need to "figure it out." You simply need to be with what is. Every time you can remember, just connect your awareness with whatever is happening in your experience. The key is to give yourself loving, gentle, and consistent reminders to show up . . . Now.

And Now . . .

. . . And Now

Just Now . . .

Right Now.

CHAPTER TWO

ATTENTION, ATTENTION, ATTENTION

*Attention is the secret of life
and the heart of practice.*
CHARLOTTE JOKO BECK

Here is my version of a Zen story from ancient Japan. One day a very rich nobleman says to himself, "Those Zen guys . . . they really seem to have life's mysteries pretty well figured out. I'm going to find out who the greatest Zen master of all is, and I'm going to go talk

9

with him." So he makes his inquiries, finds out who the greatest Zen master is, and goes to see him. Once in the Zen master's company, he declares, "I want to know all of what Zen is. I want it all formally written up, and I'll pay you for it." The Zen master replies, "Okay, that sounds great! I'll be right back." So he goes away, and, a few minutes later, he comes back with a scroll which he hands to the nobleman. When the nobleman unrolls the scroll, he sees that only a single word is printed on it: "Attention."

Puzzled, the nobleman says, "This can't be it. I want more. I want the whole thing! All of Zen." The Zen master then says, "You know, you're right. There is more." He takes the scroll and goes away again. An hour later, the Zen master returns and hands the scroll back to the nobleman. The nobleman enthusiastically unrolls it, but all it says this time is: "Attention, Attention." The nobleman becomes outraged. "There's got to be more!" he yells. The Zen master says, "You know what? You're right. There is more. Why don't you come back in a few weeks, and I'll really take my time with it and write it all out." So he takes the scroll away with him once again. When the nobleman returns many weeks later, the Zen master presents the scroll. The nobleman unrolls it, and written in large, beautiful calligraphy, he now finds the words: "ATTENTION, ATTENTION, ATTEN-TION!" Of course, then — as many Zen stories go — the nobleman is enlightened on the spot.

So, the questions we are left with are these: What is attention? And how do we practice what the Zen master is prescribing?

To understand more clearly what attention is, let's first look at what it is not: let's look at our normal state of mind. We, as human beings, are always aware. Every waking moment we are aware of something. But what is usually happening is that the content of our mind grabs our awareness, and we lose contact with our ability to be directly attentive to what is happening in the present moment. As the opinions, fears, desires, fantasies, concepts, judgments, and identities float through our mind, they "stick" to our awareness. It's as if these mental phenomena have glue on them, glue that pulls our awareness up and away from truly being in the Now.

And since this is something that happens on a very consistent basis, our awareness ends up getting "stuck" in the mind. This is the opposite of "paying attention" in the way the Zen master prescribes.

So, although we are always aware, the awareness itself is consistently being pulled into the thinking mind, the "small mind." It becomes completely preoccupied with thinking about life and identifying with being a "somebody" in relationship to life. It is continually getting caught up in the drama of our mind-made fantasies.

The Zen master in our story keeps implying: more attention, more attention. What he means is to give more and more of our awareness to the reality of life itself. And life is always, one hundred percent, happening Now, in the present moment. Therefore, as we practice the art of mindful living, we put our awareness on what is here, Now — on what we are actually seeing and hearing, on what we are feeling, tasting, and smelling. We place our loving attention on whatever is occurring to our senses in this very moment. We can call this way of attending to the present moment "attention," "mindful awareness," or simply "mindfulness."

As an example — in this very moment — you can simply notice your breath; notice the sensations in your body; notice what the mind is thinking; notice the sounds you are hearing; notice what you are seeing. Each moment of noticing is a moment of attention, of mindfulness. What we notice might not be very dramatic, but no matter how boring or how exciting it may feel, our practice is to keep bringing our awareness back to what we are aware of — Now.

I like to think of mindfulness as "the attention game." One way to play this game is to repeatedly ask yourself the question, "What am I aware of Now?" The answer to this question comes not from any form of thinking, but from directly looking, sensing, and listening. What you are aware of might be the experience of sitting in a chair, talking with a friend, or walking down the street. No matter what it is, the practice is to give your attention to it fully and directly. Just keep noticing, moment to moment, no matter what you find.

We want to bring determination and commitment to our endeavor to play the attention game — since what is at stake is the very quality of our life — but, at the same time, we want to maintain an innocent lightness about the whole thing, as if we were playing "Chutes and Ladders" or "Go Fish." We don't have to take this game so seriously that we start to believe "If I forget to pay attention, I'm bad." We want our practice to emanate from the qualities of diligence, a heartful devotion to the truth, and compassion ... not from intensity, fear, or harshness.

"Now" is always here for us to come back to; that's guaranteed. We could be asleep for twenty years and suddenly remember "Oh, yeah, my practice is to pay attention to the present moment, to Be Here Now." Whatever is going on, wherever we are, we can become mindfully aware in this moment.

The important thing to remember is that the present moment includes everything. EVERYTHING. It includes pain; it includes sleepiness; it includes aversion; it includes resistance; it includes anger. You can learn to be mindfully aware of it all. There is nothing that cannot be included in your awareness, in your noticing, in your attention. ATTENTION, ATTENTION, ATTENTION.

QUESTIONER: That can't be all there is to it. I feel like the nobleman in the story — I just don't buy that that's the whole thing! All I'm supposed to do is just notice what's happening? That will totally transform my life?

TOBIN: If you practice thoroughly, mindful attention by itself will definitely transform your life. But, actually, there is some "fine print" to these admittedly vague instructions . . . which is what the rest of our work together will be about.

For now, you can simply practice placing your attention on what's happening in the present moment of your experience. Then, to the best of your ability, you can practice "riding" that moment, like a wave. This "wave" is an upwelling of experience that is always happening, Now — an ever-unfolding flow of experience arising in the present moment. You can always catch this wave by paying attention mindfully. In any moment that you remember, you can just start "surfing"!

CHAPTER THREE

LEAVES
ON A STREAM

The difference between being in bondage
and being liberated is the difference between thinking
and recognizing that thought is thought.

STEPHEN LEVINE

As we learn to pay attention in a mindful way, we are soon confronted with the river of thoughts flowing through our mind. Learning how to relate to these thoughts soon becomes one of the most important ingredients of a skillful mindfulness practice.

As we began discussing in the last chapter, as thoughts float into our mind, our awareness "sticks" to them, and they take us for a ride: we literally get lost in our thoughts. Unconsciously, we end up believing that our thoughts are the bottom-line truth of reality just because they are going through our mind! This is called being "identified with" our thoughts. It is said that for the average person this phenomenon occurs about sixty thousand times every day.

If we pay close attention, we find that the ride these thoughts take us on goes all over the map. Some of our thoughts are of one opinion, while others are of the opposite opinion. Some are blatant judgments, while others are compassionate and loving. Some are fantasies of a hoped-for future, while others replay the past with questions of "why?" and "what if?" Some are logical and straightforward, while others are scary and fantastical.

It's not that all of the thoughts that go through our mind are totally unreliable. Some thoughts may be relatively true, may contain very important information, or may even be reflections of our essential nature. But given the current state of affairs, we clearly need a filter system so that eventually — instead of being identified with the jumbled-mess-of-60,000-thoughts-a-day we call our mind — we are free to live our life in the most true way possible.

So, the first-and-foremost, foundational, fundamental, radical shift in perspective that mindfulness meditation has to offer is this: YOU ARE NOT YOUR THOUGHTS! Your thoughts are just thoughts, just leaves on a stream.

This perspective does not imply, however, that we should try to stop or get rid of the thoughts flowing through our mind. In practicing mindful awareness, we are more interested in establishing an observing stance — in witnessing our thoughts — so that, ultimately, we become free from their power over us. In time we get to the point where we can simply notice the thoughts as they occur in our mind without getting "stuck" to them. In mindfulness meditation practice, we cultivate a different way of relating to the mind, not a way of shutting up the mind!

The metaphor of leaves on a stream is very useful in this endeavor. Other metaphors work just as well: We could play at seeing our thoughts as bubbles in the ocean, clouds in the sky, or feathers flying by in the wind. The point is to observe, to watch, to dis-identify from the thinking mind.

Let's do a guided meditation to see how this works.

GUIDED MEDITATION: CULTIVATING WITNESSING AWARENESS

Let your eyes close, and place your attention on the sensations of your breath in your body.

Now, begin to notice each thought that goes through your mind. See each and every thought that goes through your mind as if it were a leaf floating by on a stream.

Do your best not to get caught in the content, the story, the drama of the thoughts; in other words, do your best not to let them take you for a ride. When you do get "caught" by your thoughts, as soon as you recognize that you've been drifting, simply come back to paying attention to the sensations of the breath in your body. Begin again without judgment, without harshness.

Keep placing your attention on the sensations of your breath in the body. And remember, when thoughts go through your mind, simply be aware of the thoughts as thoughts . . . as leaves floating by on a stream.

Practice this meditation for 15 to 30 minutes.

Although these are simple instructions, most people find that they are not easy to follow for any length of time. Just do your best — every time you find yourself lost in thought, simply begin again, without a big to-do. Not only is it unnecessary to be judgmental or harsh with yourself when you find yourself drifting; you can actually be grateful for remembering to come back to mindful awareness.

As the saying goes, "If you fall off the horse a hundred times, you get back on a hundred and one." In mindfulness practice, this is essential advice — although, over the years, you will find it being more like "if you fall off the horse a million times, you get back on a million and one"!

CHAPTER FOUR

PRESENCE

Why not just relax and be here, simply existing in
your cells, inhabiting all your body? . . .
If you are not in your body you miss the source of all
significance, meaning and satisfaction . . .
When we are really present, the presence itself
is made out of fullness, contentment, and blissful pleasure.

A.H. ALMAAS

The value of being present in one's body cannot be overemphasized. With presence, true fulfillment is possible — without it, it's simply not. But what does it mean to be present? How do we inhabit our bodies? Aren't we doing that already?

The practice of presence is an extension of the attention practice. It is a way of bringing our attention into the body and being with our felt experience. Presence is the quality of "in-touchness," of "here-ness," of embodiment. It is about arriving in the Now, learning to show up as we live the moments of our lives.

Therefore, the practice is to inhabit your body no matter what you are doing in any given moment. While meditating, be there meditating; while doing the dishes, be there doing the dishes; while walking, be there walking; while eating, be there eating. Whatever you happen to be doing, be there as fully as possible in your body. This is presence practice — the "fullness" part of mindfulness.

Although this practice is simple and straightforward, there are many barriers that make being deeply present difficult and sometimes even impossible. It's as if there are magnets in our body . . . but turned in the wrong direction! These "magnets" seem to repel our awareness out and away from our direct experience. This can be true even in the most relaxed of circumstances, but it is especially so when there is some kind of emotional charge occurring in the body. While we can usually be present in our body to some degree, because of this "magnet phenomenon," we cannot always be as deeply present as we would like. As we place our attention in our body, we may feel only a faint sense of embodiment . . . we may even feel nothing at all.

It's important to grasp that whatever degree of in-touchness you are experiencing is okay. In order to practice presence, you need only put your awareness in your body and feel whatever sensations you have access to. The depth of presence will deepen on its own simply by experiencing your felt-sense directly — moment, by moment, by moment.

Let's do a meditation with the emphasis on presence.

GUIDED MEDITATION:
CULTIVATING EMBODIED PRESENCE

Let yourself ARRIVE. "Land" in the present moment. As in the movies, when a UFO slowly descends toward the ground and then finally lands with a thud — let yourself land here, Now.

Focus your attention on the sensations in your body. Slowly scan through your entire felt experience, starting with your head and gradually moving down to your toes. Feel the sensations in each part of your body directly as you slowly move your attention downward. Every time you get distracted, simply begin again wherever you left off.

After you have scanned through your entire body, allow your awareness to rest in the overall feeling-sense of your bodily experience.

Whenever thoughts float through your mind, practice seeing them as leaves on a stream: simply notice them and let them float away. Continually bring your awareness back to the sensations in your body, feeling your experience in the present moment as deeply and directly as possible, "riding" the upwelling flow of presence happening in the Now.

Try this for 15 to 30 minutes.

Presence — living in the here-ness of our life — catalyzes deep healing and transformation. It brings our consciousness into direct contact with what is occurring within it. This allows for us to mature and develop to our full potential. If we are not present, then we are not in touch with the experience of living, and we don't reap the benefits of what we are living through.

On another level, presence is an end in and of itself. When we are fully present, all of what we are looking for is here. Our life becomes beautiful, precious, and satisfying. You may have experienced deep presence while watching a sunset or dancing under the moonlight or making love. We usually accredit our wonderful experience to external conditions, but, actually, the joy and beauty we feel are due to our state of presence . . . a state that can become available to us anywhere, anytime.

When we are fully present — free from the filters of the conditioned mind — the qualities of satisfaction, aliveness, and magic jump off the page. They are simply in the presence itself. This experience may not be immediately accessible due to accumulated layers of conditioning that act as barriers. But — miraculously — as we consistently show up in presence, these layers of conditioning get metabolized, and our consciousness slowly becomes re-awakened to the preciousness and divinity that our life is in every single moment.

We can look at the path of mindfulness meditation as a journey toward being fully awake and embodied in our life. It is a path to our true self, our true nature, our true fulfillment. Cultivating presence is one of the main practices that propels us along this magnificent journey.

CHAPTER FIVE

A LITTLE MORE KINDNESS

You can search the entire Universe
and not find a single being more
worthy of Love than yourself.

BUDDHA

In spiritual traditions around the world, compassion and kindness are talked about as two of the most important qualities to cultivate in one's life. Jesus, the Buddha, the Dalai Lama — all the great spiritual masters — have touted compassion and kindness as the way to live. But what are these qualities, really? And how do we authentically bring them into our lives?

If we sense deeply into an experience of compassion or kindness, we can feel it as a wellspring of energy that flows forth from our Being. Each is a palpable presence, a fullness, an expression of our true nature that makes us feel warm, kind, caring, and empathic. When an experience of kindness or compassion is present, we can feel it emanating from within the depths of our heart. At the same time, we can feel it flowing into the world around us.

What surprised me in my initial experiences of deep essential compassion was that the first person who was touched by this kind, caring, loving energy was me. This came as quite a shock! My mentality was, "What do you mean . . . me? I'm supposed to be compassionate to people *out there*."

Unconsciously, I had believed that I didn't deserve compassion. So the experience of it actually welling up from my depths and touching me in such a direct way — wow! The power of that experience threw me into an exquisitely poignant realization about the nature of true compassion.

I realized that I deserved compassion and kindness as much as anyone else. And I discovered that when it does flow in myself, toward myself, freely and fully, the natural outcome is that it overflows — freely and fully! I don't have to work at being loving toward others. It just happens. It happens naturally, spontaneously, and without effort.

So, let's dive into an exercise designed to stoke the fires of compassion and kindness.

GUIDED VISUALIZATION: CULTIVATING SELF-LOVE

For this exercise, you can sit or lie down. Just make yourself comfortable.

Allow your eyes to close. Inhale deeply and hold your breath for a few seconds, then fully release. As you exhale, invite yourself to soften. Let yourself relax into presence.

Take five of these long, deep breaths. When you have finished, let your breath come to an even, relaxed, effortless flow.

Now, imagine in your mind's eye someone you love unconditionally, a being for whom you feel unconditional positive regard. Choose a being that you see as utterly precious and wonderful. It may be a child, a teacher, a pet ... whomever or whatever you can easily feel a pouring forth of good wishes, love, and appreciation for. Let yourself move close to this being so that he or she becomes vivid, more palpable, in your imagination.

Contact the sensations in your body; notice any feelings of sweetness and well-wishing that arise. Take at least a few minutes to bask in this being's presence and in the feelings you have for him or her.

Now, in your imagination, move closer and closer to this being until you are focusing in on his or her eyes. Then, let his or her face begin to slowly change into an image of you as a child. See yourself when you were a very young child. See the completely precious, totally innocent being that you were. See how this child — you — is deserving of all good things.

While you visualize yourself as a child, see if you can stay in touch with the sensations of love and caring that you were experiencing in relationship to the being you were previously visualizing.

Now, see the child that you were begin to grow up. Visualize yourself at different ages...slowly...slowly...up to the present day. Do your best to stay in touch with those same feelings of love and caring as you visualize yourself at these different ages.

Scan your body; check in with your felt-experience, especially the area around your heart; see what you feel there. As much as possible, let the quality of loving-caring permeate your experience.

If you notice any resistance to doing this, be curious about the resistance. Why is it difficult?

When you are ready, open your eyes. As you move back into your life, attempt to continue to stay in touch with any feelings of compassion and caring that you experienced for yourself during the meditation.

QUESTIONER: I could see myself as pure and wonderful as a kid, but at some point it shifted. I can't look at myself now, as an adult, and feel that same way.

TOBIN: You were pure then, and you're bad now?

QUESTIONER: That's what it feels like.

TOBIN: At some point, something happened that took away your preciousness, your goodness?! That is what many of us were led to believe. The reality is, though, that nothing ever took it away. It is not something that can be taken away. You are just as perfect now as you have always been, but you can't see it because somewhere along the way, you lost touch with this reality.

This unfortunate "fall from grace" happens to just about everyone, and the result is an underlying feeling of unworthiness. Obviously, it is very important to address and resolve this issue. But in order to do so, ironically enough, what we need most are the very qualities that seem to be most lacking — compassion, kindness, caring. Our being needs utmost care and kindness because of the very fact that feeling unworthy is so painful. We start by being as compassionate to ourselves as we possibly can be, right here, right now.

QUESTIONER: I feel so selfish going about it in the way you're describing.

TOBIN: That's a very common response. Most of us have been taught to believe that we're only lovable if we are perfectly kind and caring to others, and that if we turn that kindness and caring towards ourselves, we are "selfish." So, as we cultivate loving-kindness towards ourselves, we will often bump up against this message, as well as any other past conditioning that taught us that loving ourselves unconditionally is not okay.

I encourage you to mindfully observe any and all reactions that arise as simply leaves on a stream. See what happens if you keep cultivating compassion and kindness for yourself anyway. View it as an experiment: Continue the practice, and then wait and see if it really is selfish or not.

Ultimately, working in this way liberates the qualities of our true nature that we've been longing for all along. When our heart opens, then, in very salient ways, joy, wonder, love, compassion, peace, and ease naturally flow in our experience, and they automatically overflow into the world around us. So, allowing compassion and kindness to flow towards yourself is actually one of the most generous things you can do for the entire universe. Done thoroughly, this simple practice ends up accessing the love that is there for every being, everywhere.

Stephen Levine beautifully summed up what living a mindful life is all about in the phrase: "A little more awareness, a little more kindness." As we live our life, this can be our guiding principle. For now, I encourage you to put the emphasis on letting the kindness and the compassion be directed towards you. A little more awareness, a little more kindness . . . towards yourself.

CHAPTER SIX

SPACIOUS, ALLOWING AWARENESS

THE GUEST HOUSE

This being human is a guest house.

Every morning a new arrival.

A joy, a depression, a meanness,

some momentary awareness comes

as an unexpected visitor.

Welcome and entertain them all!

Even if they're a crowd of sorrows,

who violently sweep your house

empty of its furniture,

still treat each guest honorably.

He may be clearing you out

for some new delight.

The dark thought, the shame, the malice,
Meet them at the door laughing,
and invite them in.
Be grateful for whoever comes,
because each has been sent
as a guide from beyond.

RUMI

Like a big, open sky, our natural state of awareness is vastly spacious, receptive, and completely allowing of whatever flows through it. Mindfulness practice is about cultivating and eventually learning to re-inhabit this quality of "big sky mind."

The "inviting in" that Rumi writes about is a reflection of this openness. It is, however, extremely challenging to live in alignment with his suggestions: "Meet them at the door laughing"? "Welcome and entertain them all"? "Be grateful for whoever comes"? Easier said than done, Mr. Rumi!

Let's say you wake up one morning and you're "greeted by a crowd of sorrows." Can you imagine laughing and inviting them in? On days like these, most of us think to ourselves, "Oh my God! What's wrong with me? Am I going to feel like this forever? How do I make this go away?" Or, perhaps you wake up feeling happy — "Happiness! Great! This is just the way I like it! How do I get it to last forever?" — and then, when the happiness goes away: "Oh no, what's wrong? Where did it go? Maybe if I do such-and-such, I can get it back!"

If you watch closely, you will see that the host of your "guest house," the ego-mind, is always at the door feverishly trying to monitor who is and who isn't allowed in. At the same time, it frantically runs around trying to hold on to the good and pleasurable guests and throw the rest out. Every arrival is meticulously judged: is it a good guest or a bad one; is it right or is it wrong; is it pleasurable or is it painful?

This phenomenon is well illustrated in a classic story about the Buddha. One day, Mara, "the great deceiver of humankind," comes to the Buddha's cave to pay him a visit. At the mouth of the cave, the Buddha's attendant tries to fend her off in an attempt to protect the Awakened One: "No, no, Mara, go away! You can't come in here. This is the Buddha's cave." Mara, clever as she is, easily deceives the attendant who, although quite afraid that he's going to get in trouble, goes and fetches his master. When the Buddha sees that it is Mara that has come to pay him a visit, he simply smiles and says, "Mara, my old friend, come in, come in! Let's have some tea."

This story captures both our usual, ego-based filtering system (as symbolized by the attendant) and the attitude we're attempting to cultivate and access in our mindfulness practice: being totally open to "sipping tea with our demons."

The tricky thing is, however, that we are not Buddhas yet! No matter how many Dharma talks we've been to — no matter how many Rumi poems we've read — we find that, more often than not, we're simply not quite able to allow our experience to flow unimpeded. We're not quite able to allow the feelings of overwhelm, depression, guilt, boredom, anxiety, and pain. And it doesn't work to pretend to be okay with everything that comes our way. So what do we do?

Let's look at a specific emotion: fear. Can you have tea with fear? If fear is present, can you say, "Oh, my old friend, fear. Come on in, and let's have some tea."? Most likely, the honest answer is, "Once in a while, yes. Most of the time, no."

Of course, you can attempt to be open and spacious with fear to the best of your ability. This may work to some degree, some of the time. When it does work — great. But, typically, one feels more aversion than openness to painful or fear-based feeling states, and so, no matter how much you may attempt to open fully to your fear, you find that you can only allow it so much. In that case, there is something else you're being invited to sip tea with, which is the "aversion-to-your-fear."

If you can't simply allow your fear, the trick is to open to the aversion-to-your-fear. If you find that you feel averse to the aversion-to-your-fear, then the practice is to open to your aversion-to-your-aversion-to-your-fear. Mindful awareness is spacious enough that it has room for the fear and the aversion and the aversion to the aversion. Our practice is to be that allowing, spacious awareness that is completely open to it all.

What you will see as you practice in this way is that your so-called negative emotions will lessen and dissolve in the light of this spacious awareness. There is a paradox here, however. We are not trying to force painful experiences to go away. If we resist what comes knocking on our door, it only adds yet another layer of suffering to our experience. Resistance constricts our consciousness and makes our life feel more stuck, more heavy, more rigid.

Remember, this practice does not come easily. It is antithetical to what we, as human beings, are wired up to do. Especially as adults, we have very sophisticated, deeply ingrained modes of resisting and closing down to our experience. That . . . is why we practice. Practice, practice, practice.

After a while, you may find that you can welcome in more and more of what comes knocking at your door.

You discover that if you open, you suffer less. If allowed to flow, every painful experience comes and goes a lot more quickly than if resisted. Useful experiences can be used; old wounds can be healed; peace and ease can blossom.

Once you really understand this process, it takes on an unfolding of its own, and the deep habits of resistance in your consciousness will gradually be dissolved. Eventually, with enough patient, skillful practice, you will come to re-inhabit the natural state of your awareness, which is like a big, open sky.

CHAPTER SEVEN

LISTENING

The mystery, the essence of all life, is not separate
from the silent openness of simple listening.

TONI PACKER

Ears don't pick and choose which sounds they allow to
flow past their drums. They are open doors. Every sound
wave that happens to come their way flows right in and
is heard. One way of looking at mindfulness meditation
is as a practice that establishes this type of listening-

awareness . . . but on all fronts. We learn to "listen" to the whole of our experience, no matter what is flowing through.

Let's do a meditation to see if you can get a taste of what I'm talking about.

GUIDED MEDITATION:
ABIDING AS LISTENING-AWARENESS

Allow your eyes to close. With a receptive, open awareness, simply listen directly to whatever sounds you hear, moment to moment. Listen attentively to every sound that flows into your ears — the sound of your breath, the sound of cars outside, the sound of birds singing — whatever happens to be there in the moment. Listen as if you are hearing a piece of music that you are very interested in — that you really want to catch all the subtleties of. Listen so that you hear all the nuances of the unfolding soundscape.

Notice that the quality of listening allows for everything. Your ears don't censor things out. They are passively receptive, totally open to whatever flows into them. At the same time, notice that listening is also actively attentive. It requires your attention. Take a few moments to listen in this way.

Now, with this same passively receptive, actively attentive quality of listening, allow your awareness to include the rest of your experience. "Listen" not only to sounds, but also to the sensations in your body, to the thoughts floating through your mind, to any smells that happen to be flowing past your olfactory nerve. Listen as if your awareness were one big ear that receives "sounds" on many different levels — including sensations, smells, tastes, and the "hearing" of thoughts in your mind.

"Listen" to everything that is happening in your experience, moment by moment. If you find yourself getting distracted, simply begin again, listening freshly to the present moment. Listen as openly, as receptively, as attentively as possible to whatever is happening in the Now.

Practice in this way for 15 to 30 minutes.

Mindful awareness can be likened to a big, spacious sky. The weather floating through this sky might be beautiful and sunny with wispy little clouds, or it might be full of hurricanes and tornadoes. Either way, the sky allows. In the same way, mindful listening allows everything to float through the space of our awareness, whatever it is.

Listening is more than just allowing, however. It is at the same time interested in what is happening. Listening implies that we are giving our attention to what is being heard. In mindfulness meditation, our job is to listen attentively, with interest, with openness, to the whole of our experience in any given moment.

As you may have discovered in the guided meditation, to practice listening-awareness, you simply tune in to whatever you are aware of in the present moment: listening to the sounds around you; feeling directly the sensations in your body; "hearing" the thoughts in your mind as if they were part of the surrounding soundscape. If your eyes are open, you can also let your seeing be receptive — as is your hearing and sensing — allowing what you see to come to you.

Listening-awareness is a mode of receptive in-touchness, receiving with mindfulness the whole of the present moment as it unfolds, millisecond by millisecond. Listened to in this way, our life is a magical, miraculous orchestra, an ever-unfolding display of sense-phenomena arising and falling away . . . back into the Source from which it all comes.

Listen, moment to moment, as the music plays.

CHAPTER EIGHT

WILLINGNESS

The Key — and the name of the key is willingness.

CHERI HUBER

The art of mindful living is about learning to surf the present moment, being willing to ride the upwelling, ever-unfolding sensations of life, whatever they happen to be. To "Be Here Now" means to be here now with everything that we experience.

As we do our best to be present — to be aware, awake and in touch — we soon discover, however, that much of what occurs in our experience is not at all to our liking. In fact, we keep bumping directly into the very suffering that we were hoping to avoid by meditating in the first place! In any given moment, we might feel boredom or back pain or rage or frustration or the pain of comparing ourselves to others, or our mind won't shut up the way we want it to. For each of us, the list goes on and on.

As if all of that physical and emotional pain weren't challenging enough, in addition, we find that a great deal of resistance arises in response to these already unpleasant feeling states. On some level, we're like sea anemones. We have very sensitive "tentacles" inside, and if anything painful touches those tentacles, we automatically react with aversion . . . we become completely unwilling to abide directly in our felt-experience. We end up clamping down, literally contracting our whole being in what could be translated as, "NO! I don't want this, I don't like it, and I refuse to feel it!" We can sense this resistance as places of tension and tightness in our body. This internal reaction is usually very powerful and very automatic, and it complicates our life by adding yet another layer of pain and suffering on top of an already challenging situation.

So on this path, because much of what we meet in our experience is not to our liking, we need a certain quality to counterbalance all of this automatic aversion and reactivity. This quality is called WILLINGNESS. We need willingness when our intention to be present meets the reality of our life experience, especially when what we find there is some form of physical or emotional pain.

In the Zen center where I studied and practiced, one of the lines in the daily chants was, "Life as it is, the only teacher." We were constantly reminded that no matter what experience we were having, our job was to be with it, in the moment. Even if what we were in touch with was frustration or anger or grief or depression or rage or anxiety or pain or humiliation or jealousy or boredom or illness, we were adamantly encouraged to willingly feel every bit of what was flowing through us.

Oftentimes, I remember feeling as if I were being asked to sit in a pool of hot lava. With really intense feelings,

I would think, "No way! I can't be with this." But, at some point I was finally willing to give it a try, encouraged by the idea that "For millennia, all the Zen masters have said that this is a good thing to do . . . I guess I'll go for it."

After some time of experimenting with willingness, I realized that instead of hot lava, I could liken a really intense feeling state to a very hot hot-tub: as I put a toe in, I found that I could tolerate it, just a little. Over time, as I got past my resistance and gradually immersed myself, I found that even the most painful experience wasn't such a bad place to be after all.

The Zen masters knew what they were talking about. When we skillfully bring willingness to the moment, everything changes, magically. Our experience may still be painful or "negative," but with enough willingness and presence, the juices of our soul can begin to flow more freely. Qualities like peace, joy, wonder, and compassion can once again saturate our Being.

So, how do we actually put this into practice?

Let's say you sit down to meditate and you find sensations of pain and tightness in your neck and shoulders, and you notice that your mind is racing. Willingness practice means that you simply arrive in the moment, and feel yourself sitting there with the emphasis on feeling what is occurring in the body (which happens, at that moment, to be not so pleasurable). Willingness meets the entire experience — including the pain, the tightness, and any sensations associated with a racing mind — allowing it all to be exactly as it is, feeling it directly and fully.

In a sense, we are learning to jump on the present moment as if it were a wave and "ride" what's arising — moment, to moment, to moment. If your experience is happiness, you do your best to ride the sensations of happiness. When the happiness starts to fade, you do your best to ride the sensations of fading happiness and to be with whatever sensations are arising in their place.

Let's do a brief meditation designed to help us ride the present moment with willingness.

GUIDED MEDITATION:
CULTIVATING WILLINGNESS

This will be a very short meditation — in fact, only twenty seconds long. For this meditation, you don't have to change your posture or do anything special. Simply close your eyes, and practice willingness. How willing can you be? How open? How allowing? How in touch?

Be with what is arising in the present moment, without expectation. Notice that what is arising changes every millisecond.

Bring as much willingness as you possibly can to the felt experience in your body, whether it's pleasurable, painful, or boring. Whatever is happening, be willing to be with it for one second at a time, for up to twenty seconds. (You can even play with shortening the time-frame down to fractions of a second.)

Often, in a very short meditation like this, the ego can let go of its usual tendency to resist and avoid what is happening. Hopefully, you were able to get a taste of what willingness is like.

QUESTIONER: During the meditation, I found that an experience I usually find intolerable, a deep depression, wasn't that bad when I was willing to be with it fully.

TOBIN: When we practice with painful experiences in this way, we often realize, "It's not nearly as bad as I thought it was going to be." Consciously or unconsciously, most people have a belief that if they feel really painful emotions, they will be overwhelmed or consumed by them. The belief is that these experiences will be so painful, so excruciating, so debilitating that they must be avoided at all costs. With willingness, we often find, "I can handle this. And when I do, the feelings tend to dissolve a lot more quickly and have a lot less power over my life." Sometimes, we find that what we're in touch with can actually be interesting, even fascinating.

This isn't to say that there aren't feeling states that are simply too overwhelming or too challenging to be with on your own. In those cases, getting the support of a friend or seeking professional help may be necessary.

QUESTIONER: I experienced willingness in the way you are describing for a few fleeting seconds, but not for much longer. My access to willingness seems so transitory.

TOBIN: That's how it works. Just keep coming back to willingness, over and over and over again. The more you practice willingness, the more it will become established as a way of living. But this is a long path. It takes a lot of patient, persistent practice.

QUESTIONER: It sounds like you're talking about acceptance. What's the difference between willingness and acceptance?

TOBIN: Most of the time, with painful experiences, the bottom line is that we don't usually "accept" them. We can't make ourselves accept what is happening. However, even when we aren't accepting our experience, we can still practice willingness. We can practice willingness with our lack of acceptance — we can do our best to willingly feel into the bodily experience of not being accepting. Willingness is what authentically moves us in the direction of acceptance.

The practice of willingness implies that you are willing to be with what is happening; you are willing to feel your experience directly. "Feeling directly" is the key.

QUESTIONER: What are the rewards of all this hard work?

TOBIN: Liberation is the main reward: freedom from being run by all the unconscious forces inside of us — largely based on false beliefs and old fears — that keep us locked into a certain mode of being, a mode that creates tons and tons of suffering for us and all the people around us. That is the main, overarching reward. In addition, there are all the other qualities of our inherent potential that we talk about here: expansion, growth, joy, compassion, love, fulfillment, authenticity, and satisfaction.

But . . . it's tricky. What we are talking about is authentic willingness, not a new quick-fix formula so we can get all the spiritual goodies. Mindfulness practice is not a new-and-improved way to avoid pain and increase pleasure. That's what the ego wants to do with this practice: to make it into an advanced technique of pain avoidance.

Willingness practice is very subtle and paradoxical and, at times, very frightening. It's scary because we are learning to truly "let go" and "surrender," and we all have deeply held beliefs that are antithetical to this kind of authentic willingness. Unconsciously, we believe that we need to control and manipulate life in order to get what we want. We each have our own set of fears, issues, and concerns that will arise as we let go into willingness.

QUESTIONER: I remember when I first went to a 12-step program, there was this guy who said, "Well, let's just pray that you become willing." Since then, my life has been a journey on the road to willingness.

TOBIN: "A journey on the road to willingness": That's the journey we're all on when we do this practice.

CHAPTER NINE

TAMING THE INNER CRITIC

Out beyond ideas of
wrongdoing and rightdoing,
there is a field . . .
I'll meet you there.

RUMI

As we practice mindful awareness, one of the things we will undoubtedly notice, very early on, are all the judgments that flow through our mind. Without the ability to effectively deal with these judgments, our experience of life becomes entirely clouded and distorted.

Judgmental thoughts not observed with the light of mindful awareness have the power to derail our practice and to color our entire life experience. This is especially true of a particular brand of judgment: self-judgment. The tendency to judge oneself is one of the main barriers to living a fulfilling life — and, unfortunately, in most everyone's life, it is running the show to one degree or another.

In an insidious and powerful way, the habit of self-judgment has taken on a life of its own. It has its own voice, its own concerns, its own "reality" in our head. This tendency is so strong, so all-pervasive, and so much its own entity, that modern depth psychology has given it its own name: the superego.

The superego, also called the inner critic, is the part of our mind that holds up a yardstick and measures us against it. On the one hand, it prods us to live up to its ideals: "You better look good." "Be smart." "Become perfect." "Do it all right, or else." On the other hand, it insults us for not living up to its unrealistic standards: "You're ugly." "You're stupid." "You're a failure." "You're unlovable." As humans, we find a relatively continuous barrage of these attacks floating through our mind. It's as if a big, strong, vicious authority is in our head constantly trying — and usually succeeding — to make us feel small, deficient, weak, and bad.

It's important to recognize that within all inner-critic messages, whether they're prodding us to be better or berating us for our so-called shortcomings, is a very powerful, coercive energy that is trying to convince us of one basic thing: "You are not good enough as you are. And, in fact, you are bad and wrong." In relationship to this powerful and insidious critic, we spend a great deal of our time and energy trying to prove that who we are is indeed good enough, after all. But it never quite happens. With the superego it is always a receding horizon. No matter how "good" we get, no matter how much we accomplish, the quest to be good enough will continue because the nature of the inner critic is to continually raise the standard of expectation beyond our grasp. If we don't learn to deal with this internalized aggressor effectively, to one degree or another, we will always be at its mercy.

Each person's inner critic has its own flavor. Some are harsh and blatantly malicious. Not unlike an inner tyrant who launches vicious onslaughts of belittling, demeaning criticism on a regular basis, these types don't camouflage their attacks at all. At the other end of the spectrum are superegos that are cleverly disguised and insidiously subtle. People who have this latter type may not even know they have one. Often, these people seem successful to themselves and others. They are usually society's "A students." If you dig deep enough, however, you will find that the same underlying, very conditional, message fuels every inner critic: "You have to live up to certain ideals, and if you do, you'll be good enough. If you don't, then you are bad and wrong."

Whatever its flavor, the first thing we need to do, in the service of finding freedom from the tyranny of our superego, is to identify and expose it for what it is. We need to become aware of the inner critic as the inner critic and, in a sense, look it straight in the face and say, "I see you. I see you for what you are." With mindful awareness, we witness the judgmental content of the mind and know it as content . . . very false content based on deeply ingrained ways of thinking and believing.

We practice seeing all judgments — which includes all comparisons, "shoulds," "have-to's," and outright blatant attacks — as leaves on the stream.

Looking this entity in the face is not a pretty sight, and getting directly in touch with the underlying feelings associated with it can be a very painful process. The poignant pain of dealing directly with the inner critic, however, is quite different from the ongoing, debilitating torture one experiences while being at its constant mercy.

It is essential that we discern the attacks that are lurking within. We need to see them with as much precision as possible and expose the actual verbal messages the inner critic is using against us. Being very precise and clear about the attacks begins to drive a wedge into the whole dynamic. When you can name the attacks, you begin to dis-identify from them. And dis-identifying is a crucial part of what leads us to freedom.

As opposed to getting rid of our inner critic, mindful awareness empowers us to see it for what it is and, thus, to be free from it. Remember the scene at the end of *The Wizard of Oz,* when the Wizard yells at Dorothy and her friends, "DO NOT AROUSE THE WRATH OF THE GREAT AND POWERFUL OZ! Do you presume to challenge the great Oz, you ungrateful creatures?" Little Toto then proceeds to go around the corner and pull away the curtain, behind which is a small, insecure man standing by a control panel. "The great and powerful Oz" then yells, "PAY NO ATTENTION TO THE MAN STANDING BEHIND THE CURTAIN!" This is exactly what we are doing here. We are exposing the "man standing behind the curtain" who is masquerading as the great and powerful tyrant over our life.

As we take a closer look, we find that the "man standing behind the curtain" is made up of internalized critical voices from our past. The superego formed in our childhood, mostly in relationship to our family. The rest came from teachers, the media, ministers, peers, and anyone else who had a significant role in our life when we were young.

So, it should come as no surprise that the inner critic carries the same bitter taste as the most painful experiences from our childhood. As children, we were completely dependent on our parents or other primary caregivers to meet our physical and emotional needs. At that time the deep, unconscious belief was that if we experienced disapproval from the outside, it would threaten our very existence. As children, we are biologically wired-up to believe that — in order to survive — it is imperative that we do "what's right" to get love and approval from our caregivers. So, as a sort of internal "preemptive strike" mechanism for keeping us on the "right" path of survival-at-all-costs, we ended up internalizing any coercive energy that came our way from the outside and turning it against ourselves.

It seems almost shocking when looking at it now as adults, but as children we would do almost anything to "whip ourselves into line" so that we wouldn't meet with disapproval from the people around us. This was our naïve attempt to make it in this world. We innocently believed that we needed to beat ourselves up in order to survive. In some ways, we even turned up the intensity of the attacks so that we wouldn't have to incur the pain of what was coming at us from the outside. As adults, we have the opportunity to see the inner critic as a survival mechanism gone awry . . . and to realize that in order to thrive (as opposed to merely survive), we need to find a way to liberate ourselves from this insidiously powerful energy inside.

I want to reiterate that we are not getting rid of the inner critic — it doesn't work that way. We are practicing getting free from the inner critic's attacks on us and dis-identifying from being the one who is being belittled and beaten up. This allows us to reconnect to the inner dignity and essential goodness that is our birthright: a deep, nonconceptual knowing that "who I am is good enough, and, in truth, I am completely lovable as I am." Through this practice we discover the freedom to be ourselves — to feel alive, authentic, and dignified — without holding back, without collapsing, without cowering under the weight of this painful, internalized aggressor.

QUESTIONER: I didn't know other people had this going on, too. I thought I was the only one who was so harsh and critical towards myself.

TOBIN: This is a universal phenomenon. When you see that everybody has an inner critic, it helps you recognize that we're all in the same boat. This can feel very supportive. What's more, it can give you the perspective that you need to start questioning the validity of the inner critic's messages.

QUESTIONER: But maybe most people *are* normal, and this is just a roomful of defective people — like me!

TOBIN: Part of the superego dynamic is a belief that we need to keep it around in order to stay alive and safe. Therefore, unconsciously, we have a deep investment in staying identified with the one who is under attack, the one who is unlovable and somehow not good enough. If you look closely, you will find that, ironically, you have a very deep attachment to your inner critic!

So, as you begin to dis-identify from it, you will find a myriad of smokescreens arising to try to divert you back into the old, familiar dynamic, such as, "In my case it really is true that I am defective, and now I've just found a bunch of other defective people to hang out with!" Our conditioning makes what the superego says seem so believable. It can feel like the bottom-line truth of reality . . . that you are, in fact, not good enough and never will be unless you live up to its standards.

When it comes to the inner critic, it often happens that we'll get a little awareness of it, a little freedom from it, and then, sooner or later, it will take over once again. It's like the San Francisco fog; it keeps creeping back in, relentlessly, and clouding our vision. Or it's like ivy that won't die . . . even after you've snipped it off, it comes back when you're not looking and wraps itself around everything without you even realizing it. Therefore, we practice catching the critic in action whenever we can: "Ah-ha! It's you again! I see what you're up to. I see that this is just another way you're trying to make me feel bad about myself."

QUESTIONER: But what if I have the thought, "You're no good at meditating"? That seems to be one hundred percent true!

TOBIN: Within many inner-critic attacks, we can extract what is called a "kernel of truth." With "you're no good at meditating," the kernel of truth might be that you only recently learned to meditate, and you're really not very skilled at it yet. However, simply noting this observation is quite a different thing than judging yourself about it and believing that you should be better at meditating than you are. It is very helpful to separate out the kernel of truth from the attack. It can help us to realize that "Hey, maybe I'm not as good at meditating as I want to be, but that doesn't mean that I deserve to be beaten up for it."

The thought "you're no good at meditating" does not necessarily have an attack in it at all. The same words can be used as an attack or simply as an observation or as some combination of the two. When the inner critic is basing its judgment on an objective observation, a kernel of truth, it is much easier to buy into the attack. So it's imperative that we separate out the kernel of truth from the judgment. Sometimes the kernel of truth is easy to see, and other times it can be much harder to decipher. The judgment is always extra!

QUESTIONER: It seems like I need my inner critic. Wouldn't I be out of control without it? Wouldn't I quit my job and become irresponsible and things like that?

TOBIN: That's a concern that many people have as they begin to challenge their habitual self-criticism. When the inner-critic dynamic began, we were very young and didn't know how to take care of ourselves. So, built into the blueprint of the critic's very existence is the assumption: "You would be lost without me! Without me telling you how you should be and what you should do, you would end up just like a helpless baby again, not knowing how to take care of yourself."

QUESTIONER: But we still need to set limits with ourselves. We can't just do anything we want without consequences.

TOBIN: Definitely, there are boundaries we need to set with ourselves. But we can be responsible in our life without beating ourselves up! It's just as if you had a child who was doing something dangerous. You would stop your child, right? But, as a skillful parent, you wouldn't say, "You stupid idiot, don't do that!"

Deep inside we all have a true intelligence, an inner wisdom, that given a chance to operate, will guide our lives in an optimal way. This inner guidance enhances our ability to act skillfully and with compassion. But it requires a leap of faith. We need to muster up some amount of courage to let go of the old, familiar inner-critic-based way of living before we can reconnect to our true inner guidance.

Another thing to realize is that when we don't live according to this true source of guidance, life has a way of giving us all the consequences we need. There is a natural feedback system built into living a life on planet Earth so that whenever we are out of balance, we get the message through pain, illness, relationship struggles, and so on. This feedback system is more than enough to alert us that we need to make a change. We don't need to add inner-critic-style insult to injury!

QUESTIONER: I can't even imagine what life would be like without my inner critic. It is so familiar. It's just part of the landscape.

TOBIN: That's a good way of putting it. It does become very much a part of the familiar inner landscape. What we're doing here is contemplating what it would be like if the landscape changed. In time it can feel like the difference between being in a small, dank underground cave and being on a glorious mountaintop.

QUESTIONER: I do seem to experience the freedom you're talking about here and there, for moments.

TOBIN: Exactly, and those moments are framed by other moments. We're learning to work at the edges of those moments, to build longer, more spacious moments. Again, this isn't about getting rid of the inner critic. You can't lobotomize this part of your brain in order to feel better! This is a process that you engage in over a long period of time. We work at the edges, and over time, we experience more and more freedom and ease in our life. It's a process, not a flip of a switch.

QUESTIONER: I'm seeing a really absurd thing about my inner critic. Yesterday it beat me up for not meditating enough, and today it's beating me up for meditating too much. I just can't win!

TOBIN: Yes, it's amazing. It's insidious and relentless, and it doesn't take just one side. Actually, the only side it takes is against you — to berate you.

So, in this moment, see that those judgments are simply leaves on a stream with a lot of glue on them and that, right now, you're stuck. The goal, as much as possible, is to de-stick yourself from all judgmental thoughts, and to keep in mind that mindful awareness is the main solvent that dissolves that glue.

Although it is doable, getting free from the crippling power of the superego is quite a challenge. And, actually, when it comes to dealing with really "sticky" attacks, there are more direct forms of engaging with the inner critic that we can use in order to free ourselves. They're what I call "the second and third lines of defense." For the sake of clarity, though, I want to stay with the first line of defense, which is mindful awareness itself, practiced in a precise and thorough way. (For more on the second and third lines of defense, see "On Working with the Inner Critic" in the Recommended Resources.)

QUESTIONER: I can't believe how judgmental I am towards myself. I'm downright nasty inside.

TOBIN: That's important to see, but we want to be careful to not judge the judge. The inner critic will wrap itself around anything, even our endeavor to get free from the inner critic! We are simply becoming more and more aware of the judge — while at the same time becoming protective of ourselves — without becoming condemning of anything (not even of the fact that we will still sometimes be condemning!).

QUESTIONER: I don't feel so at the mercy of the inner critic. I seem to *be* the inner critic. I judge everything and everyone around me.

TOBIN: Although we all flip back and forth, some people are more identified with being the one who is under attack, while others experience themselves more as the aggressor. Any way you look at it, the inner critic is running the show, and it needs to be worked with mindfully.

QUESTIONER: Is the inner critic seen as an enemy, or as a wounded part of ourselves?

TOBIN: It exists in relation to a wounded part of ourselves; it is beating up a wounded part of ourselves. It's trying to protect us, to help us survive, but it's doing so by using our own power in an aggressive way against us.

In this dynamic it is the wounded, small, defenseless, vulnerable part of ourselves that is continually getting attacked.

So, I wouldn't necessarily call it an "enemy," but I would call it a "bully." If you saw a seven-year-old kid in the park beating up on two-year-olds, you wouldn't necessarily see that kid as an enemy, but you're damn well going to do something to prevent him from thrashing the little kids. It's the same in relation to our inner critic. There needs to be a point when we say, "No more! This is not okay."

QUESTIONER: This work seems impossible to me. There are just too many judgments, too much of the time.

TOBIN: That's when it's particularly important to do this work! It may be difficult, but that doesn't mean not to do it.

And it is certainly not impossible. It just may seem that way in the beginning. But the more intense your inner critic is, the more it behooves you to really do something about it.

The inner critic can take over our entire life experience. It completely robs us of knowing who and what we are, making it impossible for us to appreciate ourselves and enjoy our lives. In a way, seeing it as a robber of our life (or as a bully beating up on a young child) is crucial, so that we will rally the energy to say, "No more — this needs to stop!"

When we're identified with the inner-critic dynamic, it's as if we're in a prison cell with our head stuck in between the bars, so that we don't even see that we're being held captive. What we're now learning to do is to step back and see the bars that are keeping us locked up. These bars are the specific messages that our inner critic feeds us on a consistent basis. We need to see these messages clearly in order to free ourselves from their power over us.

When one is free from the tyranny of the inner critic, there is a one-hundred-percent powerful experience of positive regard for oneself. We then know that any harshness that comes our way is blatantly untrue and something that we need to protect ourselves against. We remember, beyond any shadow of a doubt, that in our very nature we are truly precious, perfect, and lovable.

CHAPTER TEN

DHARMA SOUP

It doesn't work to try to develop one aspect
of essence without the others . . .
Only the development of all the qualities
will enable us to become full, true human beings.

A.H. ALMAAS

The qualities we have been discussing so far — attention, presence, compassion and kindness, spacious-allowing-awareness, willingness, witnessing awareness, and the strength and dignity to work diligently with the inner critic — are what I consider the "essential ingredients" of a skillful mindfulness practice. It's as if our life is a big cooking pot and we're looking to make a rich and delectable meal to nourish the quality of our existence. These essential ingredients are like the foundational ingredients, the stock, to which we can add many other qualities — for texture, for flavor, for balance — until we find just the right blend to serve our life in the deepest way possible. This artfully blended concoction of qualities is what I like to call "Dharma Soup."

"Dharma" can be translated to mean "the Way" or "the teachings of the Living Truth." The process of making Dharma Soup is the fine art of bringing what we learn about the Living Truth into our life — into our formal meditation practice, as well as all the activities of our everyday life: into walking and talking and eating and sleeping and working and relating and struggling and getting into the thick of things.

The essential ingredients are just some of the many skillful means we use to help us on this journey. In addition, we need other qualities such as diligence, perseverance, lightheartedness, humility, curiosity, passion, gentleness, earnestness, patience, concentration, relaxation, and intelligence. At the same time, we need for all of these qualities and ingredients to be balanced in the right proportions. Dharma Soup is like any other soup; if you have a lot of one ingredient and not enough of another, it doesn't taste right.

For example, the quality of diligence is vital to a successful practice. But if what motivates our practice is primarily diligence, our life can take on a rigid, "tight" quality. If it isn't balanced with an ingredient like compassion or gentleness, we can get "lopsided." It's the same with the quality of loving-kindness, which needs to be balanced with strength — especially a protective kind of strength — for those times when we need to defend ourselves against the inner critic. Or the quality of devotion — a deep, sincere commitment to one's path — this needs to be balanced with lightness or a sense of humor about the whole thing. Another example is the "witnessing" quality that allows us to dis-identify from our thoughts and from the content of our experience; this needs to be balanced with presence, or embodied awareness. In other words, while we definitely want to be clear and open like a sky, we also want to be deeply grounded and in touch with the earth.

When creating your own personal pot of Dharma Soup, it's important to realize that you can rarely have too much of any one ingredient. However, if you do have a lot of one quality, you will most likely need to balance it with a lot of its complimentary quality. For example, take the quality of passion: the ardent desire to live your life in the most meaningful, liberated way possible. The more passion you have, the more you will need to balance it with practical intelligence — a clarity of mind that takes your entire life situation into consideration, not just what you're passionate about. Passion can be likened to the fuel for our path, and intelligence to the fuel injectors that help monitor the flow of fuel into the right places, in the right amounts, at the right time. Too much fuel without good fuel injectors can lead to a real mess!

The ingredients aren't usually talked about in this way. For instance, in the Zen story from chapter two, the nobleman is instructed by the Zen master to pay "attention, attention, attention." Although the essential ingredients are implicit in these instructions, for most people, simply being told to pay attention is not specific enough to create a balanced, skillful practice.

For most of us, making the qualities explicit (that is, getting precise about what ingredients make for good Dharma Soup) makes all the difference in the quality of our path and can serve as helpful guidance through-out our entire journey. This has been crucial for me over the years. When I first began my practice, I was quite intense and determined; unfortunately, I was also rigid. It wasn't until I began cultivating compassion, lightness, and childlike curiosity that I experienced an authentic softening and balance, which not only felt better, but also helped my journey to unfold and evolve in a much more efficient way.

So, if you feel out of balance in some aspect of your life, you can ask yourself, "What's missing in my soup right now? What am I not including?" You can become the gourmet chef of your own life — a dash of this and a dash of that!

QUESTIONER: This all sounds great, but unlike carrots and vegetable broth, if you don't have an essential ingredient, you can't just go and pick it up at the grocery store. If you don't have some needed ingredient, how are you supposed to get it?

TOBIN: Good point. Often, just realizing that we're out of balance helps us to access more of the ingredient that we need. But this is certainly not always the case. So what do we do then?

Let's say that the ingredient you recognize you need and want more of is relaxation — the ability to chill out and soften into your being. First, you can cultivate the quality by practicing relaxation techniques, by remembering to relax as often as you can, or by any other creative approach that works for you. But too much effort or "trying to relax" will be antithetical to your goal. At that point, what you can do is to discover and work with any barriers that are in the way of relaxation occurring naturally and spontaneously. You can begin this exploration by earnestly inquiring into these questions: "What is in the way of me being more relaxed in my life?" "Why is it difficult for me to simply relax?" This discovery process alone is very helpful. In addition, once you have seen a barrier, you can apply any skillful means at your disposal — which might be anything from a very simple mindfulness technique to a more in-depth process like therapy — to help dissolve it. When the barriers are seen and dissolved, the authentic quality is naturally more available.

The same goes for any quality: the two main things you can do are (1) cultivate it and (2) be curious about and work skillfully to dissolve whatever is in the way of it. This entails some sincere work, as the obstacles blocking access to these qualities can involve deeply ingrained conditioning affecting our whole way of being. Secondly, it requires courage, as one of the root barriers to embodying any given quality can be a deep-seated fear that living more deeply from that quality will threaten one's familiar sense of self and therefore — ultimately — even one's very survival.

QUESTIONER: Is there any quality that counterbalances willingness?

TOBIN: Willingness is one of the most important ingredients in our soup, but without "Right Action" — or

Skillful Responding, as I like to call it — it is lopsided. So, along with huge amounts of "willingness to be with what life presents us," we need equal parts "Skillful Responding." This involves using the deepest intuition we can access to act in the wisest way possible in any given situation. To help with this, we can ask ourselves, "How can I truly serve here? What would be the most skillful thing I could possibly do in this situation?"

Willingness, if not balanced with Right Action, can lead us to being overly passive in our life. If we don't watch out, we can end up becoming a doormat, willing to be the receptacle of whatever gets dumped on us. This is definitely not what willingness is about! With every situation, there is a skillful action that wants to flow forth . . . even if that action is to confidently sit there and do nothing.

QUESTIONER: I have a question about this balancing act between willingness and Skillful Responding. When I'm feeling certain kinds of pain, there is an impulse to get up and flee or to do something else "productive." I think this is my ego . . . or maybe it's my intelligence. I don't know if I should just be willing to continue to be with my feelings or if I should get up and deal with the situation.

TOBIN: Your question reminds me
important ingredient needed in our Dha
ingredient is discernment — looking for
a discriminating eye.

Obviously, though, clear discernment is not always easily accessible, especially when it involves discerning what
action to take. For example, with the situation you're
struggling with, sometimes it's best to stay with painful
feelings; other times it may be best to move away from
them. In any given situation, all you can do is decide for
yourself by applying your deepest discernment to the issue with as much integrity and intelligence as possible.
If you practice living with as much discernment as possible in each situation, then, over time, your capacity for
clarity will develop. For now, experiment; with as much
refinement as you can muster, do what feels most true
for you and see what unfolds. Aim in the direction of
what feels right; pay attention to the results, and learn
as you go.

But let's be careful . . . One of the potential pitfalls of
Dharma Soup practice is that once we know what the
ingredients are, we can get it into our mind that we

should always be those ways. If we don't watch out, knowing what the ingredients are can become fuel for the inner critic. The true motivation for all of this work comes from a heartfelt, intuitive knowing that one's true nature lies in the direction of these qualities, and, therefore, one wants to live from them in a fuller way. This needs to be approached in a very authentic way. If it's at all forced or faked, it is better to let it go for the time being and return to the practice of simple, mindful awareness.

Ultimately, when we talk about Dharma Soup, we're talking about finding the "Middle Way." And the Middle Way can be very difficult to find and even more difficult to live from! It's like a slippery ridge — an icy precipice with troughs on either side — that we can easily slide into and get caught in.

For instance, in the case of willingness and Right Action, on one side of our slippery ridge is the state of rigidly believing that we "know" how reality should unfold and trying to control our life according to this strongly held belief. On the other side of the ridge is the state of being lackadaisical and flippant about life. Notice how both of these options are distortions of what true willingness and Right Action are. That's what happens when our conditioned, fear-based sense of self — in other words, our ego — is running the show. Whereas, the Middle Way, our proverbial slippery ridge, is the place where there's an authentic willingness to be with life as it is and, at the same time, an ability to act skillfully.

Most people tend toward either one side or the other of any Middle Way, any slippery ridge. If you're the kind of person who usually lives from the attitude of "I know how reality should look and feel, and it should always be just the way I think it should," then your ego-mind has taken over, and you're hanging out in a trough. In that case, you can experiment with moving in the direction of willingness and hanging loose a bit. Whereas, if you're someone who is so "willing" all the time that you sit around not engaging assertively in your life circumstances, and you've seen that this is your pattern (that is, you've seen that this is the trough you tend to hang out in), then you can experiment with taking more intentional, skillful action.

EXAMPLE OF A MIDDLE WAY
"Willingness" Balanced with "Skillful Responding"

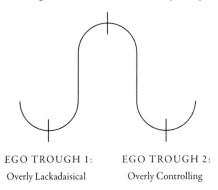

EGO TROUGH 1:
Overly Lackadaisical

EGO TROUGH 2:
Overly Controlling

This is just one example of a slippery ridge that we run into as we engage in a committed mindfulness practice. Along this journey, life presents us with countless opportunities to practice aligning with the Middle Way. As we add the different ingredients to our soup, we artfully attempt to strike a balance — oftentimes between two seemingly opposite qualities — in a way that is ultimately paradoxical but, at the same time, completely satisfying and totally natural to our soul.

QUESTIONER: Whenever I try to walk the Middle Way, I become very indecisive, and then I lose the opportunity to act. I get so focused on wanting to take the Middle Way that I get stuck.

TOBIN: So, we're seeing that one of the troughs that you fall into is trying to do it so right that you don't do anything at all. It sounds like you have "Right Intention," which is an important ingredient in anybody's soup. Keeping in mind that you don't need less of any skillful ingredient, you want to balance it with increasing the level of something else . . . which, in this case, would be "spontaneity" or "having trust in yourself" or "willingness to make mistakes."

QUESTIONER: But that's hard to do. Life goes so fast!

TOBIN: It is very hard! Just give yourself the space to go through the learning process of becoming more and more spontaneous over time. For that to happen, you will probably need to err on the side of "going for it." And you will also need to practice "eating the red-hot coal" of fear (see chapter eleven) that is standing in the way of your freedom to act spontaneously.

There is one last ingredient I want to mention in order to balance all of the details and precision we're getting into here, and that is the quality of simplicity. If all this talk about making Dharma Soup and learning to walk the Middle Way gets confusing, or if you find yourself getting caught in your mind trying to "figure it out," you can just let it all go. Simply do what you feel would serve you — what you intuit would be best for you at this time — without a big to-do. Let simplicity be your guide.

Simply do your best, and let go of the rest.

PART

TWO

WORKING WITH
DIFFICULT EMOTIONS

Anger . . . sadness . . . hatred . . . frustration . . . guilt . . .
rage . . . fear . . . loneliness . . . humiliation . . . hurt . . .
grief . . . lust . . . anxiety . . . resentment . . . worry . . .
restlessness . . . depression . . . overwhelm

Wave upon wave of difficult emotion moves through us.
No matter how much we may try to avoid it,
much of what we find flowing through
our experience is charged with reactivity.
Learning to skillfully work with these painful
waves of emotion is one of the most important
components of living a mindful life.

CHAPTER ELEVEN

EATING
RED-HOT COALS

The aim of practice is not to develop an attitude which allows a man to acquire a state of harmony and peace wherein nothing can ever trouble him. On the contrary, practice should teach him to let himself be assaulted, perturbed, moved, insulted, broken and battered — that is to say, it should enable him to dare to let go of his futile hankering after harmony ... that he may discover ... that which awaits him beyond the world of opposites... Only if we venture repeatedly through zones of annihilation can our contact with Divine Being, which is beyond annihilation, become firm and stable.

KARLFRIED GRAF VON DURCKHEIM

A big part of the path of mindful awareness is learning to embrace and directly feel our painful emotions. With willingness, we practice saying yes to the waves of feeling that move through us. We practice being as fully present with them as possible, and as we do, we find that our awareness has a miraculous, transformative, healing power to it.

When our awareness is allowed to touch the emotional wounds inside us, directly and fully, true healing and resolution can finally take place. This healing process is rarely easy, however. It takes a great deal of courage, compassion for ourselves, and patience.

Biologically we are wired up to move away from pain and toward pleasure. So when strong, painful emotions arise, the instantaneous, knee-jerk reaction is to resist feeling them. Ultimately, this aversion to feeling pain is an important survival mechanism. However, it has one very big limitation: In our rejection of whatever triggers the feeling of pain, we end up rejecting the painful feelings themselves. This presents us with quite a problem, since whatever painful feelings we are not able to allow and directly experience get repressed in our psyches and tend to wreak havoc in our lives!

The consequences of this phenomenon are profound and are evident everywhere we look — in how we feel about ourselves, in how we experience our life, in our relationship dynamics, and in the dynamics of the world at large. Therefore, learning to be with our pain — especially our emotional pain — in a skillful way is crucial for healing on all of these levels. That makes this one of the most compassionate and loving practices we can do, not only for ourselves but for everyone, everywhere.

I call this aspect of our mindfulness practice "eating red-hot coals," and I must admit that the prescription here is bitter medicine. In the long run, however, this remedy is well worth taking.

A common expression for emotional reactivity is "getting our buttons pushed." We each have our own unique set of buttons that get pushed in relation to specific triggers. We are probably only too familiar with the kind of experiences in which seemingly custom-tailored situations or people continue to show up in our lives and evoke strong emotional reactions in us. What psychodynamic theory (not to mention enough personal experience) shows us is that these buttons inside of us do not get randomly pushed. Instead we find that the buttons themselves are acting as very powerful magnets that magically pull people and situations into our lives that will end up pushing them. Miraculously, we keep getting into the same kind of relationships with the same kind of people who do the same kind of things, over and over again. And in response — much to our dismay — we keep having the same familiar feelings of frustration or overwhelm or jealousy or suffocation or fear of being abandoned. As we start to explore our patterns of reactivity, we may be surprised to discover that most — if not all — of our painful emotions are actually a response to these "magnetic buttons" getting pushed.

This magnetic-button phenomenon works in a variety of ways. The main way is that it draws people and situations into our lives that replay unresolved past experiences. For example, if we were repeatedly yelled at as a child, we may unconsciously be attracted to, and thus draw into our lives, a partner who verbally abuses us. But that's not the only way these buttons work. With this type of childhood background, we are also going to be conditioned to readily perceive others to be verbally abusing us when they may not actually be doing so. To further complicate matters, we will also have an unconscious tendency to "pull on" the people in our lives in such a way so as to replay the wounding from our past that has yet to be healed. For instance, someone with whom we are in relationship, who may not normally be inclined towards yelling, may find themselves uncharacteristically losing their temper with us due to the pull being exerted upon them by our subconscious.

The variations on this theme are almost infinite. In addition, they are very complex and are totally unique to each person. And, no matter how hard we try to avoid it, until we learn to eat our red-hot coals, we will keep encountering the same familiar situations and types of people that will keep triggering us in the same frustratingly familiar ways, over and over and over again. This is a profoundly powerful force that is way beyond our conscious control.

As we take a closer look at these magnetic buttons, we discover that they are the result of unhealed emotional wounds. These wounds are caused by painful experiences that have happened to us in life, usually in childhood. As children we were very sensitive and vulnerable. Many of the painful experiences that happened to us felt like they were literally too much to handle. Because we believed that these experiences would overwhelm and annihilate us, as a survival mechanism, we repressed the emotional pain connected to them. In a sense, we said "NO!" to these experiences with such force that we ended up shoving them out of our awareness and deep into our unconscious. Consequently, these intense emotions got "stuck" in our psyches.

So now, as adults, we have these undigested emotional wounds sitting there, "pulsating" in our unconscious. And even more troubling is the fact that these encapsulated pockets of unhealed emotion have become very powerful magnets that mysteriously attract (and make us more sensitive to) people and situations that are custom-designed to trigger those same painful emotional responses.

It's as if our soul got all scraped up in childhood, and we have left the wounds under bandages ever since. In this practice, we learn to take off the bandages and let the air

of mindful, compassionate awareness finally reach —
and ultimately heal — our inner wounds.

Let's do an exercise to get a sense of how we can mindfully work with our painful emotions.

GUIDED PRACTICE:
CULTIVATING MINDFULNESS
OF EMOTIONAL WAVES

To begin, bring your attention into your body as fully
as possible.

Scan slowly through the entire field of your body. Feel
your feet and legs . . . slowly move your attention up
into your hips and belly . . . next, feel your back and
chest. Then, bring your awareness into your hands . . .
your arms . . . your shoulders . . . your neck . . . and face.
Be as in touch as possible with whatever sensations you
become aware of as you feel into your body. Take your
time, allowing yourself to slowly sink into presence.

Once you feel relatively present in your body, bring to
mind a recent situation that triggered a strong emotion

in you. As you replay the scene in your imagination, be mindfully aware of whatever sensations flow through your body. Do your best to feel the waves of sensations that move through you. Stay with the felt-experience as directly as possible, for as long as possible.

When the emotion subsides, replay the memory once more. Again, feel the sensations in your body. Allow the waves of sensation to flow through you, and pay very close attention to the entire process that unfolds in your experience. Practice being open and curious about the details of your experience as it unfolds, moment by moment.

The trick here is to allow whatever experience you are having to happen, to simply deepen your connection with it, being curious about the entire unfoldment and, at the same time, doing your best to willingly feel whatever is happening in your body in a mindful way.

QUESTIONER: This seems ridiculously hard. When my buttons get pushed, the experience in my body is gut-wrenching. I really don't want to feel it directly.

TOBIN: That's exactly why this part of the practice is called "eating red-hot coals." This is the painful, somewhat brutal, part of our path. Literally the last thing in the world we want to do is to mindfully be with these experiences. And then, even when we have decided to embrace this practice, we find that, especially with really intense feelings, our awareness is like oil on a hot skillet: as soon as it connects with the sensations, it skitters off again into distraction or thought. Often, we are able to stay present with our painful experiences for only a very short time, sometimes as little as milliseconds.

These red-hot coals are what we have been trying desperately to avoid our entire lives. We will do almost anything not to feel them intimately! So if this practice is especially challenging for you, go slowly. "Touch in" to your painful emotions for a few moments at a time, without forcing yourself to go beyond what feels doable in any given moment. This is a gradual, ongoing process. With diligence and devotion to the practice, you can always revisit the feelings at a later time.

QUESTIONER: In the guided imagery exercise, I didn't really "feel" any emotion. My mind kept trying to put a label on my experience, trying to figure out what I was feeling. Do you have any suggestions for getting more in touch with the felt-experience?

TOBIN: The felt-experience is always happening in the Now, at the level of sensation. When an emotion is flowing through, you can simply pause for a second and dip into it with your awareness. You might feel it as tingling in your fingers or a zap in your chest or heat in your face or surging energy in the trunk of your body. There are an infinite number of ways that we feel our emotions. Simply go to the felt, visceral experience. Over time your ability to sense mindfully will deepen naturally.

Of course, the mind will continue to do what it's wired up to do. For a long time, it is going to want to run the show. When we are having an emotional reaction, we will probably have more thoughts than usual, and they may feel more real than ever — more sticky and more believable. So when we are feeling reactive, it will be especially hard to see thoughts as simply thoughts, just leaves on the stream. Nonetheless, that is our endeavor: to see each and every thought as a leaf and then to put our attention down into the body. Right here, right now. You might be able to do this for only a very short period of time, but that's okay. Just keep coming back to your felt-experience, again and again.

QUESTIONER: I felt some kind of anger, but I'm not sure if it was really anger. When I was with it, questions started to arise about whether it was anger or something else.

TOBIN: In a way, it doesn't matter what you call it. What does matter is that you feel it in your body. That's the key. The label of anger can be helpful if it brings you back to the felt-experience. But when you're in touch with your immediate experience, it's beyond all labels anyway. Each time you feel angry it will be different. And if you really pay attention, even within one experience of anger, you will see that the sensations are changing all the time. The key is to experience the sensations as they unfold, whatever they happen to be. Then you are truly supporting your soul's unfoldment.

QUESTIONER: What about crying? I felt tears welling up. Is it okay to cry?

TOBIN: Crying is fine. Wailing is too, if that's what is flowing through you. Just remember to feel the emotions in your body as you are having them.

QUESTIONER: It's almost like letting the body speak its unspoken words.

TOBIN: Yes, and the body's language might not always be a voice. It might be an experience of terror, sadness, or rage.

QUESTIONER: The body's language also includes joy, right?

TOBIN: Definitely. It includes joy, peace, bliss, and all the other pleasurable feeling states you can think of. And you will find that you actually have a lot more joy the less you resist all the states that don't feel like joy.

Ironically, for some of us, extremely pleasurable emotions can be even harder to allow than painful ones. Whatever arises, be it pleasurable or painful, our practice remains the same: allow and feel directly whatever is happening.

QUESTIONER: In the exercise I felt so much resistance to being with my feelings. The whole thing felt like pure suffering to me.

TOBIN: Remember that our biological impulse is to move away from pain. The thing that tends to cause the most suffering is our resistance to being directly with our pain. The resistance itself is the suffering. If you let go of it and you move into your pain in a more and more immediate way, it's just sensation; it's just pain. It's not nearly as bad. But if we step a tenth of an inch outside of our painful feelings and we try to push them away, that's when the suffering begins. It's our attachment to not having painful experiences that turns our pain into suffering.

This distinction between suffering and pain is crucial. Every time you move your awareness into your felt-experience, you suffer less, even if it's the most excruciating pain in your back, or some tremendous emotional turmoil you're going through. So, ironically, as we learn the art of being in touch with our pain, we actually decrease our suffering. (If what you are getting in touch with is based on serious trauma, then there is a wisdom in your biological impulse to move away from the over-whelming sensations. Learning to dip into this kind of emotion bit by bit is actually a very fine art that is best approached with the help of a skillful guide. For a recommended book dealing with this subject, see "On Working with Trauma" in the Recommended Resources.)

QUESTIONER: It seems like it takes forever to heal these wounds. I've been doing this practice for years, and even though things have changed in my life for the better, sometimes I still get caught in the same patterns.

TOBIN: Do you remember those massive jawbreak-er candies? When I was a kid, I remember thinking, "There's no way I'll ever finish this thing!" I could go through layer after layer after layer and still have a huge jawbreaker left. But if I stuck with it, lick after lick after lick, at some point it was gone. Every time we work with our emotions, it's like a lick on a jawbreaker. You think it'll never be gone, but if you keep going . . . no more jawbreaker.

In this practice we are learning to be with each layer as it reveals itself. And as we work with the layers mindfully, we go deeper and deeper into ourselves, and we get closer and closer to healing the deepest aspects of the wounds inside. In time, even though the wound might still be there, the depths of our soul slowly become more transparent to us, and these — instead of being painful pockets of undigested emotion — are deep wells of the qualities inherent to our natural state of Being: peace, joy, gratitude, love, intimacy, and so on.

As always, it is important to remember not to try to "get rid of" your jawbreakers. This is a subtle art, not a new self-improvement project. The best approach is to surrender to the practice of eating your red-hot coals every time you have an emotional reaction.

QUESTIONER: So are you saying that with enough practice we won't have emotions anymore?

TOBIN: No, not at all! I'm saying that deep healing can happen. We will still have emotions, but they will be much more spontaneous, much more appropriate to what is actually happening in the present situation. They will flow through us more naturally and be let go of more freely. Once we heal the emotional wounds from our past, life in general becomes a lot less problematic; our actions become more aligned with the wisdom and compassion of our true nature instead of being driven by emotional reactivity.

But, typically, this process does take time — a long time. Much longer than it takes to lick through a jawbreaker! It's helpful not to get attached to being rid of your wounds; they might be with you a lot longer than you'd like. Hopefully, though, just knowing that mindful awareness has a healing effect is enough to motivate our practice. Then, with a lot of patience, gradually our life is completely transformed.

Something else to keep in mind is that you don't have to fully heal these wounds in order to experience freedom from them. At some point in the process, you find that even though your buttons still get pushed, they are not running your life any more. Along the way miracles happen, shifts occur, and profound gifts are received.

QUESTIONER: I just broke off my marriage after ten years. It has been hellish. How do I work with the emotions around this situation in the way that you're describing? It seems too intense.

TOBIN: With something as big as what you are going through, the key is compassion. It is very important to be caring and kind with yourself and not to push yourself beyond what is doable for you at every given point.

Sometimes feeling an emotion can be like getting hit by a meteor directly in the guts. Ultimately, you can learn to sit there and take it a little bit at a time, gradually opening to the experience fully. If that is too much for now, then you can consciously move away from it for the time being, or you can seek professional help.

So when you ask how to work with your particular situation, the answer is to do your best and try to remember that the practice isn't to "get over" your emotions or to be "past them" already. Sometimes in this life, huge waves of pain do arise whether we want them to or not. Practicing mindfully means that we let ourselves feel these waves as much as we possibly can. At the same time, it is vitally important that we bring a loving intelligence to the whole process.

QUESTIONER: I have a hard time telling if my wounding is from my childhood or from the current situation, especially in relationship to my wife. What she does actually seems harmful to me.

TOBIN: Often, the current situation is so well designed that we are easily convinced that the wounding is coming solely from the present. It is more likely, however, that the current situation is causing wounding on top of wounding — wounding that occurred long before we ever met our partner. And it tends to go both ways. As much as we hate to admit it, our partner is most likely experiencing some type of wounding that he or she feels we are causing!

Love relationships have a particular way of triggering our issues. You can pretty much guarantee that every painful emotion that comes up in a love relationship is connected to some wounding from the past. This, counterintuitively, makes it an ideal setting for healing our red-hot coals. The key lies in a devoted use of our awareness and choice. It is one of the most challenging — and at the same time most rewarding — practices that we can engage in. It requires a fierce dedication to in-touch awareness combined with an uncompromising willingness to shift our focus.

It starts the moment that our partner sets us off. In that moment we (1) become fully aware of the sensations of pain that we are experiencing. We then (2) catch ourselves in the act of wanting to blame the present relationship or act out in some old, familiar way. We (3) choose to see those impulses and all the thoughts that go along with them as leaves on the stream and let them float by. Then — and this is the pivotal shift — we (4) make the conscious choice to change our focus to one of curiosity about the past: "What past situation of overwhelming pain has this just brought me in touch with?" Once our focus has shifted to curiosity about the true source of the pain, we (5) allow ourselves to experience the pain directly, with the knowledge that as we do so, we are using the experience to process a wound from our past in order to free ourselves of its effects on our life.

We may need extra support in our endeavor to make this type of radical shift in the dynamics with our partner. Couples counseling can be extremely helpful in this regard. In fact, I feel no couple should be without it, at least at some point in their relationship.

Another important point to make here is that if things really are abusive in your current situation, you should not hesitate to do whatever it takes to remove yourself from harm's way. The point I'm making is that the original wounding came from the past and that the deepest healing resides within you . . . but, at the same time, taking responsible and dignified action in the current situation is also vitally important.

QUESTIONER: Do we need to figure out where the wound came from? Do we need to track it back to the original source?

TOBIN: Insights about the origins of your wounds may spontaneously pop up. If that happens, great. If not, that's fine too. Just keep doing the practice.

With a particularly sticky pattern, establishing yourself in mindfulness and doing a meditative inquiry can be helpful. In meditative inquiry we use the mind in conjunction with meditation to unearth the roots of what is going on. Inquiry can be very, very useful and can greatly help our process to unfold. It is an art form that we can develop over time.

For now, it's enough to understand that when your buttons get pushed, it's time to eat those red-hot coals. It is difficult, bitter medicine, I know. But I also know how liberating it can be. Like nothing else, it has the power to change your entire life, from the inside out.

CHAPTER TWELVE

THE GATELESS GATE

The "secret" of life that we are all looking for is just this: to develop through sitting and daily life practice the power and courage to return to that which we have spent a lifetime hiding from, to rest in the bodily experience of the present moment — even if it is a feeling of being humiliated, of failing, of abandonment, of unfairness . . .

When we rest at peace with our suffering,
this repose is the gateless gate.

CHARLOTTE JOKO BECK

We have been exploring a vital part of our mindfulness practice — the fine art of feeling our feelings. Inevitably, however, whenever I say "feel your feelings," just about everyone has the same response: "I've been feeling these feelings for years! That's why I'm coming to see you, so I don't have to feel them anymore." So, let's take a closer look at the fine line that exists between this usual kind of "feeling" our feelings and the meditative practice that I have been describing. Understanding this crucial difference will help us to open to our emotions and let them impact us in a way that leaves us truly transformed.

When we mindfully observe our feelings, we find that what we usually call an "emotion" is actually a combination of things, including thoughts, sensations in the body, and some amount of resistance to feeling those sensations. It is helpful to separate these elements out from one another so that we can more clearly see and skillfully work with the waves of emotion that flow through us. For instance, when someone says, "I'm feeling angry," they are probably experiencing a combination of the following: (1) a slew of thoughts floating through the mind that are being believed and identified with, (2) waves of sensation in the body, and (3) an aversion to feeling those sensations. That whole package of thoughts, identification with the thoughts, sensations in the body, and resistance to feeling those sensations is what most people would call "feeling angry." The same goes for sadness, overwhelm, anxiety, frustration, humiliation, hatred, depression, and so on.

As we begin to tease apart these various components, one of the first things we see is how compelling and believable all of the thoughts are that go along with our feelings. For example, say someone close to you forgets to call you on your birthday, and you feel "hurt." With a feeling state like this, you may find many thoughts floating through your mind such as, "what an insensitive, uncaring person she is" or "I am so unlovable, of course she forgot to call me." These thoughts are the leaves on the stream that we discussed earlier. With an intense emotional experience, the thoughts can be very convincing and feel totally realistic — in other words, they can be very sticky, tenacious, poison-ivy-like leaves. They are invariably rooted in conditioning and wounding from the past, rather than in anything that is happening in the present situation.

With any given emotion, we also find — happening concurrently with the thoughts in our mind — a whole array of sensations unfolding in the body. Changing moment to moment, these sensations flow like a river through the space of our awareness. With mindful awareness we experience this as a current of feeling that we might call trembling, heat, surging energy, contraction, vibrations, prickles, or pain. With some emotional experiences, the sensations have a "denseness" to them; with others, they feel ethereal. Some feel soft, almost imperceptible, like a subtle flavor or feeling tone in the background of our experience. Others feel intense, like a volcano that shakes us to the core. However it may feel, every emotion can be experienced as a wave: a flow of sensations in the body. For example, with anger there might be a tightening of your muscles and heat in your chest and arms. With sadness, you might find a teary quality behind your eyes and an aching in your chest. With frustration, you might feel like your skin is scratchy and tight, as if it is two sizes too small for your body.

In conjunction with these powerfully sticky thoughts and the flow of accompanying body sensations connected to almost any emotional wave, we will also find some deep resistance to whatever painful sensations may be arising. In addition to our biological aversion to pain of all kinds, we all have incredibly deep, powerful fears about what it would mean to experience our painful feelings directly. Therefore, almost invariably, we find that resistance is a part of the ball of wax that we call an emotion.

So, to mindfully feel our feelings, we practice seeing our thoughts as thoughts, and we remember that these thoughts are just leaves — just mind-stuff — to notice and let go of to the best of our ability. Then we work with our resistance: We may not like what we are feeling, but we practice being willing to be with it anyway. We then place our attention on the flow of sensations unfolding in our body, deeply and directly, moment to moment.

Let's look at some examples. Say you're meditating and the thought goes through your mind: "Oh my God, I have so much to do tomorrow. I have a list a mile long, and I don't have enough time to do it all." If you're paying close attention to your body as these thoughts float by, you will probably notice that, along with them, comes a flood of sensations: tingling, vibrations, tightness in the chest — a whole pattern of sensations instantly flows forth like a geyser.

As a more challenging example, say you get into an argument with your spouse. This will likely bring about a much more intensely charged experience than having a few thoughts about your busy schedule, triggering many more long-lasting, tumultuous waves of thoughts, body sensations, and resistance.

Things get even more complex if you are experiencing something like depression. With a feeling state like this, there may be layers and layers of emotion — waves upon waves of thoughts, resistance, and body sensations — that are happening chronically in certain patterns, both consciously and unconsciously.

With all of these emotional experiences, what is of utmost importance is to keep coming back to the sensations in the body, whatever they happen to be and, with as much diligence, patience, and willingness as possible, to feel them fully and directly. Obviously, experiencing our emotions in this way may not be one bit pleasant! When you're in the midst of eating a red-hot coal, it definitely does not feel like freedom or expansion or liberation. It is, however, the doorway to these qualities.

In Zen they call our direct experience the "Gateless Gate," a portal to the truth of who we really are. And, often, in order to enter this portal, we have to be willing to sit in our painful, sometimes hellish, emotional experiences.

Willingness to be present with our experience is what helps us to access the Gateless Gate — the place where authentic healing and liberation happen; the place where we experience deeper and deeper levels of truth, of reality, of ourselves. When we practice skillfully with our emotions, when we feel them directly, we go through a metamorphosis process that leaves us transformed in a fundamental way.

QUESTIONER: I've been feeling sad for months, but this week I had an amazing experience in which I finally let go of trying to get rid of my grief. I said to myself, "Okay, if this is here forever, I'll accept it. I'll be with it."

And the amazing thing was — that's when things started to change! I couldn't believe it.

TOBIN: That's exactly what we're talking about. When we practice saying yes to even the deepest kinds of hurt, our process can then unfold. Transformation is a natural outcome of this type of openness and allowing.

However, true openness and allowing is not thinking, "I'm going to say yes to my experience so I can get rid of it." This is just a more sophisticated version of what we have been doing all along — rejecting our experience! Which only serves to keep all of our wounding and suffering in place.

QUESTIONER: But how do I trust that my pain will go away? What if it just keeps getting worse and worse?

TOBIN: Unconsciously, to one degree or another, we all suffer from a lack of trust that if we let things be, our lives will unfold in a positive way. We all have beliefs such as, "If I allow my painful emotions and the situations that are causing them to be as they are, then they will just get worse and worse and will end up taking over my life." Because of these deep fears and lack of trust, we have a very hard time allowing ourselves to simply relax into our experience.

In reality, though, it is resistance that makes things worse. When we resist our emotional wounds and the outer circumstances of our life, we get more entrenched in our pain and, consequently, have a harder time discovering what is best for us. Ultimately, it is our fear, resistance, and lack of trust that get in the way of our life unfolding in an optimal way.

Letting our feelings be as they are and simply feeling them can be a bit scary (not to mention downright terrifying) until we have some experience with this process. Once we see that the habitual ways of rejecting our experience and trying to force life to be other than it is aren't working, we may feel ready to let ourselves and our feelings simply be. This readiness is not quite trust, but in the beginning it is enough to go on. Over time, by experiencing the power of this practice directly, trust will build naturally.

Something else to keep in mind when we first start working with our red-hot coals — especially since we have spent years and years closing down to our emotions — is that for some period of time we can expect for things to actually feel worse in some ways before they feel fundamentally better. Imagine a river that has been dammed up for a long time. Once the dam is lifted, the current is going to be extremely strong before it settles down to a natural flow. We may not be aware that we have had so much unprocessed emotion built up inside. We may just sense that something isn't feeling right in our life or that we keep getting thrown into similar frustrating situations that push our buttons in painfully familiar ways. So when the unconscious accumulation of repressed feelings is finally allowed, seen, and felt, we will most likely feel worse before we feel better.

QUESTIONER: I feel like I've been practicing being present with my emotions pretty well. I practice and I practice but it seems to be taking forever, and sometimes it's hard to know if things are really changing. It's getting pretty frustrating.

TOBIN: Personally, in my own practice, I wasn't aware of any major shifts for a long time. I didn't feel any Gateless Gates — or any of that wonderful mumbo jumbo

— for many years. I had so much built-up rigidity, so many layers of tension, from so many years of anxiety, stress, and conditioning, that for a long time in my practice all I could do was learn to be willing to be with all of that, as it was.

For most of us, before there are Gateless Gates and portals and essential experiences, a large part of our practice is about being present with our conditioning. One helpful way to think of it is that we are "melting ice cubes." When you're melting ice cubes, what you're aware of, for the most part, is the ice . . . not the melting. It might feel — for quite a while — as if mindfulness practice is not working at all. That's because as you begin to engage in this process, you become more aware of the ice and you most likely will not be able to feel the melting, let alone the deep goodness of your being that lies on the other side of it. But if you stay with the process and you're willing to feel your feelings directly, over and over, then melting happens. It's a universal law that if you put heat on ice, it melts. It's the same with our inner ice: as you apply the heat of mindful awareness, it melts. The process just takes longer than we want it to, and for some time we can't see the reality of what is happening.

Here in the West, most of us were brought up in a very fast-paced culture, where we were able to get whatever we wanted fairly quickly if we just applied enough effort (or at the very least, we were taught that that's how life should work!). The message was that if we applied enough effort, we should be able to get everything we want right away. In the journey of mindful awareness, we will find ourselves bumping up against this conditioning because the transformation we're talking about here happens according to a very different timeline than the one we are used to dealing with. I like to think of it as the "soul's timeline." The Dalai Lama, for example, has said to look at your progress in decade-long time frames.

Although this practice is miraculous and things do change dramatically, you may not see the results as quickly as you would like to! In fact, the shifts can oftentimes feel very slow and grueling. That's why the quality of willingness is so important. Willingness implies that we are doing something that we don't necessarily want to do, but we intuit that it's in our best interest, so we do it anyway.

I hope that I'm making clear the important difference between the usual understanding of "I'm feeling my feelings" and what we are talking about here: labeling the thoughts, working with the resistance, and experiencing directly the sensations of our emotions as they are happening in any given moment. The latter is the pathway through the Gateless Gate.

By wholeheartedly embracing this practice over time, we find that it opens us to the qualities that we have always longed for, the qualities of our true nature. We come to realize that emotionally charged experiences are actually portals into another dimension . . . a dimension of beauty, wonder, peace, and authentic joy.

CHAPTER THIRTEEN

SKILLFUL RESPONDING

Do you have the patience to wait
Till your mud settles and the water is clear?
Can you remain unmoving
Till the right action arises by itself?

LAO-TZU

Practicing mindfully with our emotional reactivity is very challenging, to say the least. Anger, jealousy, hatred, fear, frustration . . . each of these feeling states creates a powerful surge of "energy-to-act-out" that is custom-designed to get us to do something: to try to make somebody be different than they are, to fix the situation, to change ourselves, or to get away from whatever is triggering us. Basically, these intense emotions motivate us — they kick us into gear! — to do whatever we can to make the pain go away.

Biologically, our emotional reactivity is designed to help insure our survival, to get us to act quickly and effectively when danger is imminent. To that end, these emotions erupt with tremendous energy, and when they impact us, everything in us goes into action mode so that we can find our way back to safety and a sense of inner calm. Psychologically, this boils down to us wanting to do whatever it takes to make ourselves feel better. So, any trigger that makes us feel threatened (physically or psychologically) will set off a powerful surge of feeling that is itself both very painful and at the same time very motivating. When we are feeling this type of reactivity, anything feels better than being mindfully present with these powerful waves of emotion!

The problem with this dynamic is that most of the time (unless there really is a threat to our physical safety) what our strong, painful emotions motivate us to do doesn't match what we would do if our highest wisdom, our deepest intelligence, were guiding us. Action that emanates from conditioned reactivity usually does nothing but exacerbate whatever problem we are having, making things worse for us and all the people around us.

Because the knee-jerk actions that we feel compelled to do out of our reactivity rarely serve us or anyone else, as part of our mindfulness practice we want to learn to "rein in" our habitual, emotionally based actions. By doing so we discover that we can have a huge wave of intense feeling without having to act on it. Instead, we can simply feel it. This is true even of the most intense feeling states. Fireworks and volcanoes can be happening inside of us, and yet we can keep ourselves from acting out in the automatic way the emotion would dictate. Ultimately, this frees us to live a life of authenticity, spontaneous goodness, and deep wisdom.

In essence, we are talking about the difference between reacting and responding, and it's important to have a precise understanding of this difference. As human beings we have the capacity to respond to life, to act skillfully in relationship to what we come in contact with. True responding comes from a place of inner freedom and a feeling of oneness where our sole motivation is to show up in a way that is best for the entire situation at hand. Whereas, when we are coming from conditioned, emotional reactivity, our sole motivation is to make ourselves feel better in that moment.

Deep inside there is a wisdom that, if we learn to let it guide us, can optimize our life. When we learn to live according to this "inner knowing," our entire life flows with much greater ease and harmony. Once we have reined in the knee-jerk action that wants to flow out of our emotional reactivity, we can start to look for this wisdom, our true source of inner guidance. Once we access it, we simply do our best to act in alignment with it.

Let's look at a simple example, say, when someone cuts you off on the freeway. If you pay close attention, one of the first things you will likely notice is that a bunch of judgmental thoughts quickly flood your mind. At the same time, you will probably feel a volcanic explosion of sensations in your body. These intense sensations and the judgmental thoughts work together, creating a powerful energy that makes you want to lash out. I call this energy "the hundred horses," and depending on the situation, it can have a ton of force behind it.

As part of the path of mindful living, we practice "reining in" these hundred horses. We rein in this energy not so that it will go away, but so that we don't create further suffering in us and in the world around us. As opposed to acting out of that energy, we feel it directly in the body as it is happening. We "burn with it," breathe into it, experience it, and bring our curiosity to it. This is the "eating red-hot coals" practice and, as we've seen, it can be intensely challenging, especially when the hundred horses are chomping at the bit!

Next (after we have reined in the hundred horses, eaten our red-hot coal, taken a lick on our jawbreaker, and melted some of our ice cube!), we move into the situation with whatever skillfulness we can. We do our best to take whatever action feels like it would be most true and healing — the action that is in alignment with the deepest intuitive guidance we are able to access in that moment.

QUESTIONER: These reactions happen so fast! How am I supposed to stop myself?

TOBIN: Often, things happen so fast that our conditioned reactivity gets the best of us . . . the hundred horses are quick and powerful, and we are in the habit of letting them loose. But at some point, if we're committed to living a more liberated and authentic existence, we remember: "Oh yeah, I want to rein in the hundred horses and all that stuff." Right then and there, we do our best to practice with it.

If the hundred horses are too fast and powerful to rein in — if you do lash out and cause mayhem — then, if at all possible, you can apologize, clean up the mess you made, and commit to doing your best from that point on. If your intentions are sincere and you are committed to this practice, at some point a shift will happen. You will become more and more skilled at being with whatever intensity is moving through you instead of lashing out. Over time, this drives a wedge into the momentum of habitually acting out of our reactivity. We can then act from our highest truth. And since our buttons are getting pushed all the time, we will have no shortage of opportunities to practice this with!

QUESTIONER: I wonder, though, about not being a doormat. One time, a car came barreling around a curve and almost hit me. At the bottom of the hill, I stopped the driver and said, "Look, I realize it was accidental, but you almost killed me. You need to be more careful." I felt really good about that.

TOBIN: Like I said before, when we get to a point where our reactivity isn't running the show, then we align ourselves what would be the best thing to do in the situation at hand. If the answer is to inform someone of something, even in a strong and assertive way, then that's what we do.

So, the approach I'm suggesting is not at all about being a doormat! It's not about being "Mr. or Ms. Spiritual," who does nothing but watch their mind and feel their sensations. Right alongside the watching of the thoughts and the feeling of the sensations, we act in whatever ways feel most appropriate, most "true," at the time.

When we get to the part of the practice where it's time to take the most appropriate action, sometimes it will be to do this thing or that thing, and at other times it will be to do nothing. But the skillful response will never be one of blaming or attacking. And it's never going to be "make the other person understand how they should be at all costs." When we are caught in conditioned beliefs, we may think, "I've got to teach this person a lesson. Since I know how reality should be, I've got a duty to yell at this guy and tell him what a horrible person he is."

That is never the skillful thing to do.

In time this practice frees us to take wise, spontaneous action. But first, most of us need to slow things down enough that we can discover the skillful response. We may be so used to being habitually run by our emotional reactions that for a while it is best to err on the side of doing nothing, until we can act from clarity. For those whose tendency it is to be more complacent, more "doormat-ish," it can be important to nudge things in the direction of assertiveness and spontaneity.

QUESTIONER: Are you saying we should never just let our anger flow? What about expressing ourselves?

TOBIN: There's nothing wrong with expressing your anger; it's just how and when you do it that matters. It is important to communicate how you feel, and to take care of yourself, but not from the waves of reactivity. When feeling emotionally charged, it is usually best to wait until the emotions have cooled down a bit or have been worked with to some degree, so that skillful communication can happen. Depending on the situation and one's skill with this practice, the time to wait could be anywhere from weeks, to tenths of a second.

As we've discussed, the internal pressure to lash out is very intense! It's as if a bone is put right in front of us, and there's a hungry pit bull inside that wants nothing more in that moment than to chomp on it. I'm talking about resisting the urge to chomp; choosing, instead, to directly experience the sensations that arise in your body (including the voracious urge to chomp), and then, when the time is right, doing your best to take whatever skillful action you can. In some situations, you will still want to act with strength, conviction, or intensity, but it is important to be able to discriminate between authentic — albeit strong — action and emotional, ego-based reactivity.

In addition, you can find a sheltered situation and express your feelings to your heart's content. In the privacy of your own room or out in nature, you can yell, hit things . . . really let it rip. It can be very fruitful and, ultimately, very liberating to let it all out; what we give expression to can find its peace and be let go of. A teacher of mine once said, "Let it all flow, so you can let it all go." This is another art form that can be mastered over time. It helps us to filter out the intense charge in our emotional reaction and get to whatever clarity resides on the other side of it.

QUESTIONER: I've never done a "mindfulness practice" before, but I think I already do what you're talking about to some degree. I feel like I'm pretty good at impulse control and not acting out in my life.

TOBIN: That can be an important place to start. But what I'm talking about here is something much deeper than just impulse control. I'm talking about all the — subtle and not-so-subtle — ways we cause harm out of our reactive habits of behavior and conditioning. Ultimately, this is about refining our ability to catch even the most miniscule ways that our fear-based conditioning — and the familiar sense of identity that goes with it — causes us to live in ways that are harmful to ourselves and others. Over time, we become liberated from this programming and can live in alignment with the true flow of the Universe.

Also, it's worth taking a closer look at what we're calling impulse control. This can sometimes masquerade as something else: a fear-based, conditioned response that is all about repressing ourselves or trying to "do the right thing." This causes us to shut down to our experience and actually become unresponsive. This is the opposite of what we're cultivating here, which is the ability to open to our experience and directly feel the sensations that accompany it, while at the same time aligning with a response based on a deep inner guidance. Ultimately we are finding the freedom to act — to act spontaneously and fully — from our innate wisdom as opposed to our emotional reactivity and habitual patterns of behavior.

Another subtle possibility to watch out for is that even when we exercise impulse control outwardly, the same energy-to-act-out may be propelling us to "act out" inwardly. In other words, we may be beating ourselves up, frantically trying to "figure things out," blaming the people or circumstances around us, or unconsciously suppressing our feelings with such force that they end up leaking out in other ways. These tendencies need to be worked with mindfully, compassionately, diligently . . . in the same way we work with our outer forms of reactivity.

In Buddhism they call this Right Action or Wise Action. I am calling it "Skillful Responding." Regardless of what name it is given, it is a crucial element in the art of mindful living. As we work mindfully with our own emotional reactivity, it slowly loses its power over our life, and we gain access to a true source of guidance, a deep intuitive intelligence. Action that flows from this place serves us and the entire world around us: we become conduits of true wisdom and compassion.

We don't need to wait until we're totally free of our conditioning to practice in this way. We can practice Now, with every situation that comes our way. Over time, our actions become aligned with our innate clarity. Our lives flow with more ease. We leave a wake of goodness and love wherever we go.

CHAPTER FOURTEEN

EMBRACING OUR AUTHENTIC HUMANNESS

Just sit there right now
Don't do a thing
Just rest.

For your separation from God, from Love,
Is the hardest work in this world.

HAFIZ

Inspiration is a wonderful thing. When we read books on spirituality or hear a good Dharma talk, we get to peek behind the veils, so to speak. We get a glimpse of what's possible. Like sipping fresh, clean spring water, it is pure refreshment — an encouraging boost that few experiences can match.

When we're talking about the art of mindful living, it's a very different matter. It is one thing to sip the pure, sweet water of inspiration and quite another thing to swim in the — sometimes calm, sometimes rough — currents of our life in such a way that our soul is deeply transformed.

As great as inspiration is, after we put the book down or we leave the Dharma talk, it won't be too long before we, once again, meet up with our own nitty-gritty life circumstances. This is the very terrain we need to go through on the way to seeing beyond the veils! And for every single human being on this planet, this terrain involves struggle — a great deal of struggle. It has its ups, and it certainly has its downs. In other words, it has its waves . . . waves upon waves upon waves.

When it comes to the struggles, problems, and difficulties of life, the normal personality mode is to emphatically push them away, to try to make them disappear.

We just want to transcend! But, much to our chagrin, we find that the authentic path of transcendence can happen only by swimming through the very muck we've been trying to avoid all along. The genuine spiritual journey is the journey of embracing our life as it actually is . . . messy challenges and all.

That's not to say that there isn't — right alongside the struggle — a lot of joy, beauty, love, and bliss. On this path the two go hand in hand, creating a positive feedback loop. In time, we discover that embracing, grappling with, and healing our emotional struggles is what brings about deeper embodiment of authentic liberation. And, in turn, we find that these experiences of liberation will, at some point, expose the next layer of emotional blockage that needs to be released. As we skillfully navigate through that layer, with its painful feelings and constrictions, we will once again feel a sense of liberation and inner peace. As a result, we relax into ourselves even more, and eventually the next layer of inner wounding is exposed. And so on, and so on . . .

As we open to our life experiences — no matter how deeply painful or challenging they may be — our life becomes a creative discovery process in which, layer by layer, we blossom. Each layer that is shed in the process becomes a doorway to a deeper experience of truth, and our inherent potential is revealed.

The right perspective is critical to effectively supporting ourselves through this journey. Getting caught in the trap of believing that "I should be liberated already" or that "because I've had an experience of deep peace, I should always feel that way" is the best way to derail our process altogether. Freedom is a gradual process of unfoldment that happens as we open our hearts to and embrace our authentic humanness.

QUESTIONER: But so many people seem like they have it all together. I've always thought that I'm the only one who has so many struggles in life.

TOBIN: We live in a culture where we are conditioned to "look good" and act like we have it all together. This is very powerful conditioning. It creates an entire culture of people who, to one degree or another, end up looking like they've got it all together. In addition, we are wired up to fixate our attention on the people who seem like they have it "more together" than we do and not to even "see" the rest of humanity. So through this filter, it's easy to look out into the world and think, "Everybody has it together. They don't struggle; they don't complain; they don't have health problems, relationship issues, work dilemmas, or money fears."

But, the more deeply you look at the reality of life on planet Earth, the more you realize that all people are given their share of challenges and painful experiences. At some point along this path, what we come to accept is that if we have a body and we are living on this planet, then the terrain we're moving through is one that is going to be fraught with pockets of suffering and struggle.

So, to be on a spiritual path in an authentic way, we need to learn to embrace and work with the nitty-gritty reality of our life. It's as if we're growing a glorious garden. If we stay directly with the process, with our feet on the ground, our hands in the mud, doing the sometimes grueling work that needs to be done, then the garden grows, the roses bloom, and the fruits ripen on their own.

Our soul is such a garden.

RECOMMENDED RESOURCES

ON MINDFULNESS AND MINDFULNESS-RELATED PRACTICES

Everyday Zen: Love and Work by Charlotte Joko Beck

The Presence Process by Michael Brown

Any book by Pema Chödrön

Any book by Thich Nhat Hanh, especially:

> *The Miracle of Mindfulness: An Introduction to the Practice of Meditation* and *Peace Is Every Step: The Path of Mindfulness in Everyday Life*

Any book by Cheri Huber, especially:

> *The Key: And the Name of the Key Is Willingness; There Is Nothing Wrong with You: Going Beyond Self-Hate;* and *The Fear Book: Facing Fear Once and for All*

Any book by Jon Kabat-Zinn

Any book by Jack Kornfield, especially

> *A Path with Heart: A Guide Through the Perils and
> Promises of Spiritual Life*

Any book by Stephen Levine, especially

> *A Gradual Awakening*

Any book by Toni Packer, especially

> *The Wonder of Presence: And the Way of Meditative
> Inquiry*

The Power of Now: A Guide to Spiritual Enlightenment
by Eckhart Tolle

ON WORKING WITH THE INNER CRITIC

*Soul Without Shame: A Guide to Liberating Yourself from
the Judge Within* by Byron Brown

*Taming Your Gremlin: A Surprisingly Simple Way for
Getting Out of Your Own Way* by Richard Carson

ON THE SECOND AND THIRD LINES
OF DEFENSE

Finding Freedom from Your Inner Critic (audio)
by Tobin Giblin

ON WORKING WITH TRAUMA

Waking the Tiger: Healing Trauma by Peter Levine

ON REALIZING YOUR TRUE NATURE

Any book by Adyashanti

Any book by A.H. Almaas, especially:

> *Diamond Heart, Book One: Elements of the Real in Man* and *Essence: The Diamond Approach to Inner Realization*

ABOUT THE AUTHOR

 For over two decades, Tobin Giblin has wholeheartedly dedicated himself to spiritual awakening and serving others in the blossoming of their highest potential. Utilizing a variety of modalities, Tobin helps individuals, couples, and groups bring about deep, true, long-lasting transformation. His work addresses issues on the spiritual and psychological levels to help people reach an experience of genuine fulfillment and settled satisfaction. His main areas of expertise include relationships, work, stuck patterns, life purpose, and spiritual embodiment in the midst of everyday life. Tobin acts as a catalyst for positive change, helping to clarify and align an individual, couple, or group with their highest potential. He is a master at helping people identify and work through any barriers that are standing in the way of this blossoming. Tobin works in a variety of potent and creative ways to bring about an embodied, liberated, and joyful spirituality.

Tobin can be reached at 415.283.8925.
www.TOBINGIBLIN.com

PRAISE FOR TOBIN GIBLIN

"I have been meditating for almost a decade now, in a variety of different traditions, and guided by many great masters, pundits, and Dharmas. And yet, my time with Tobin this last week, in silent retreat, was a revelation. Specifically what did I walk away with? A newfound juicy joy in meditation . . . a sense of resting, of literally not doing anything, and not just bathing in Silence as Love but actually becoming that profound unmovable pervasive Silence that is Love . . . I am forever grateful."

~JAMES W.

"Tobin has given me immeasurable help in transforming my life. Since we began working together, the difference in my life is like night and day. Thank you, Tobin, for your unfailing support, for your integrity, and for your example. There really are no words that could do justice to the depth of gratitude I have for you."

~HEATHER A.

"Working with Tobin has helped me to quiet the storm of mental distraction and land in the calm of the present moment."

~CHRIS B.

"I'm really at a loss for words when I feel into how grateful I am for your love, guidance, support, wisdom, compassion, and caring . . . You are masterful, and I mean that in the truest and fullest sense of the word . . . You have amazed me with your ability to so delicately and precisely attune to exactly what my being is in need of in each moment in this tricky and paradoxical journey of conscious awakening. It is clear to me that you have emerged from your own journey with an open and full heart that is ready and willing to serve others in their blossoming."

~DAN K.

Lightning Source UK Ltd.
Milton Keynes UK
UKOW031853180413

209453UK00012B/574/P